How to Utilize Your Mind

Through the Science of

Practical Psychology

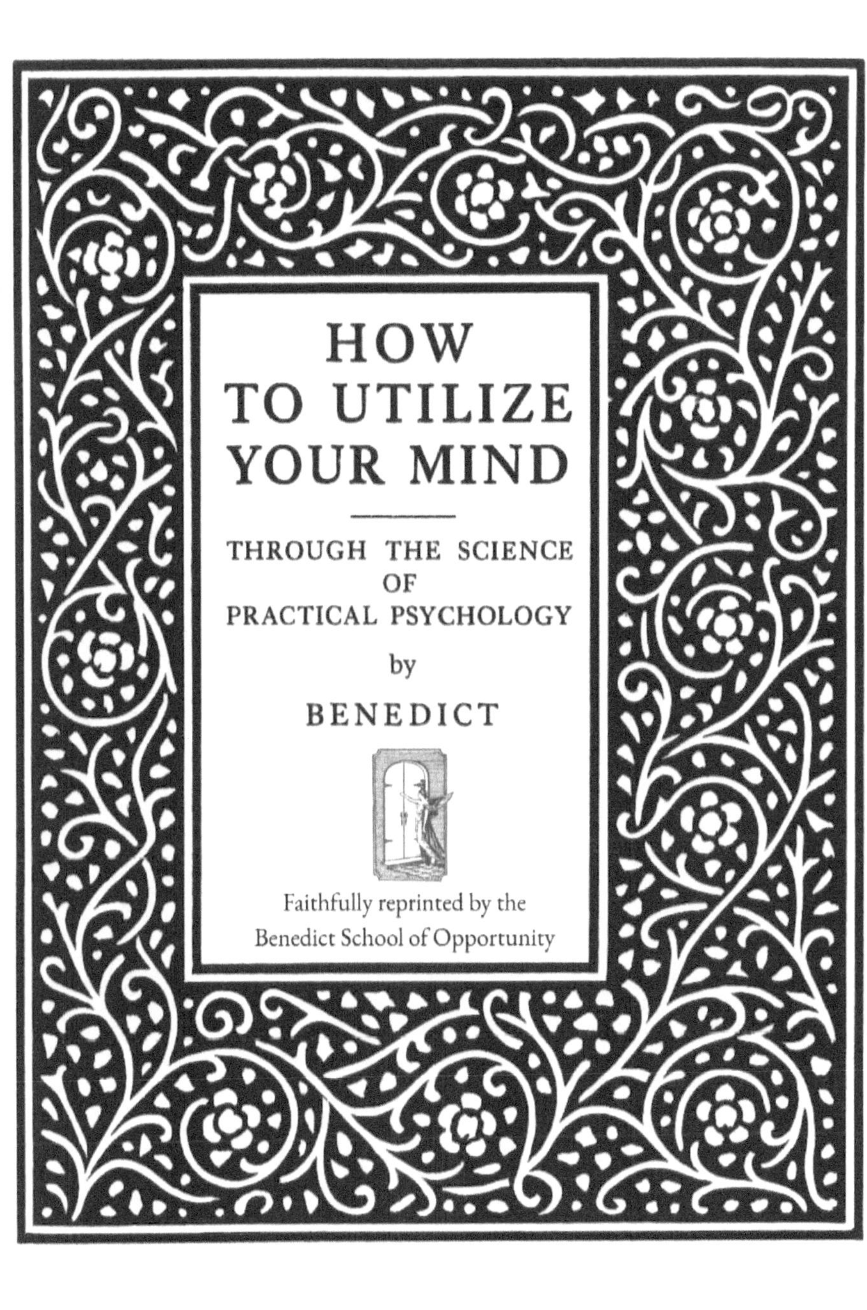

HOW TO UTILIZE YOUR MIND

THROUGH THE SCIENCE OF PRACTICAL PSYCHOLOGY

by

BENEDICT

Faithfully reprinted by the
Benedict School of Opportunity

CONTENTS

DEDICATED
TO
OUR STUDENTS

How Your Mental Attitudes Control Your Life

We build our future thought by thought,
For good or ill, often know it not—
Thus so the universe was wrought.
Thought is another name for fate;
Choose then thy destiny—do not wait—
Knowing love brings love and hate brings hate.

—Ella Wheeler Wilcox

ONCE, with a group of other tourists, I was standing on the rim of the Grand Canyon when a portion of the embankment near us gave away and went crashing to the bottom.

Several people screamed; others exclaimed, "Oh, how sudden!" But it was only the **culmination** that was sudden. Seepage, weathering and decay had been at work many years underneath those tons of apparently normal earth.

Whether or not underground disintegration is going on in you can be determined by your answers to these questions:

What Are You Doing with Your Life?

Are you getting somewhere?

Are you self-reliant, optimistic and glad to be alive? 🙠🙠

Are you brimming with energy, health and buoyancy? Or are you only half alive, with something always wrong?

Are you so magnetic that it is an inspiration just to see you?

Are you dominating your environment or is it crushing you?

Are you a slave to worry, timidity and fear? Or are you master of your moods?

Can you use your mind for what you want it to accomplish for you at any time regardless of disturbances? ❧❧

Do you remember things, or is your memory a cluttered junk heap where you can't find anything when you want it?

Is your will power nothing but wish power?

Are you getting flabby, old and dumpy, or holding your own with Father Time?

Do you live to eat, or do you know how to eat to ***really live***?

Do you know how to make the money you want, or are you always "too poor to afford it?"

Whoever you are

Whatever you are

Wherever you are—remember this:

In every man and woman there are enormous untapped resources. You are using only a small percentage of yours. You are like a ***hundred-acre field with but ten acres under cultivation.*** If you doubt this, you are cheating yourself.

What You Are Doing

You are letting Discouragement, Worry and Fear grip you and ruin your life when you could be happy ❧❧

You are letting yourself get old when you could stay young and attractive.

You are doing all kinds of things to your body that make you ill when you could be well and strong.

You are timid and self-conscious when you could be radiant with self-confidence.

You are a FAILURE when you could be a SUCCESS ❧❧

A Matter of Knowing How

But determination alone will never change your life. Knowledge has always been necessary to accomplishment. The will to solve a problem is useless without the KNOWING HOW.

There is a key to joyous, successful living, based on natural laws.

This course in Practical Psychology explains these natural laws, with special reference to their effect upon mind and body and their interactions as shown in health, worry, confidence, memory, will power and money-making.

It puts into vivid, graphic form the psychology of the great universities and applies it in everyday language to the everyday problems of everyday people. It is the psychology and biology of the greatest and most recent scientific discoveries made understandable, helpful and above all PRACTICAL.

Where Will You Be At 65?

Statistics show that:—

Out of every 100 healthy people 36 die of preventable diseases before they reach the age of 65.

Of the 64 out of the 100 who live longer—

1 will be rich,

4 will be well to do,

5 will be earning their own living,

54 will be dependent on relatives, friends or charity ❧❧

Man A Part of Natural Law

With human beings as with all other things, there is a *cause* behind every *condition,* a *reason* for every *result.* There is an internal, mental side to every external physical effect.

Man is not apart *from,* but a part *of* natural law. His only chance of being happy or successful lies in his understanding and utilizing these natural laws in relation to himself and his personal problems &

Superstition belongs to the dark ages; the notion that illness, sorrow, or failure descend upon you from outside of yourself or from a Creator desirous of "punishing you for something" is as false as it is foolish.

The Mind and The Man

No man is bigger than his mind.

The differences between those who succeed and those who fail lie in the *differences between their minds.* Happiness, the one deepest desire of every human being, the end and aim of all work, sacrifice and aspiration—is nothing but a *state of mind.*

The difference between the happy man and the sad one is never a difference in external things, but in *internal* ones. The man with a million may be miserable, while the tramp walking down the road may be happy. This one priceless possession—the "bluebird of happiness" each of us is hunting for—is hatched nowhere save in our own minds.

Mental Attitudes

The most vital things in your life are your mental attitudes. Your life at this moment is but the *massed result* of the mental attitudes of your yesterdays. Nothing "just happens" to you. Everything happens in accordance with law and the biggest law in human life is that of mental attitudes. &

There Are No Accidents

We see things happen which we think are "accidents," just as the child thinks it an accident that a thing drops to the floor when he lets loose of it. When he grows up, he learns that it was caused by the eternal law of gravitation.

We are but children—babies in our ignorance of the forces that rule life and the universe. But the race is gradually growing up, slowly but surely learning a few more laws, the greatest of which are those of *mind and its effect on our lives*

Mind and Matter

We are learning that though some things are material, tangible, and concrete, they act and react in accordance with unseen forces, and that the same condition invariably causes them to react the same way.

We are learning through the science of Practical Psychology that though our muscles are definite material things they are powerfully influenced by our minds.

We are learning how the mind affects health and why it is that we lose all physical weariness the moment some exciting or thrilling thing we WANT to do comes along.

If we dislike to do a thing we are tired before we start; the very thought of it makes us weary. This and a hundred similar experiences will prove to the most casual thinker how power fully his mind affects his body.

Explain These

Why is it so hard to get up on week days when you HAVE to go to work, but so easy to get up early on Sunday, Christmas, and the Fourth of July?

How was it that as a youngster you could be too sick to go to school, and twenty minutes after nine be well enough to go hunting with dad?

That time you had a "splitting headache" what became of it when your best beau phoned and asked you to go to the theatre?

What became of your appetite when you received a telegram containing sad news?

Why does the entire world look different when you fall in love?

Why does the day seem black and empty when your loved one flirts with somebody else?

What becomes of your sleepiness when interesting company arrives?

Why do you get so sleepy so early in the evening when the company IS N'T interesting?

How can you work so late and hard at a thing you like and feel just as good the next day as if you had had a complete night's rest?

Why do you forget all about being thirsty or hungry or tired or sick whenever anything exciting happens?

Why is it no work to get up a big dinner for people you like but a toilsome task to do it for people you don't care for?

How is it that you never seem to have time when it's just the family, but plenty of time to "spruce up" when a guest you are *interested in* is coming?

Why does a horse travel so slowly when being driven away, but speeds up the instant you turn his head toward home?

In these cases, and thousands of others every day, the whole thing depends on your *state of mind.*

> *"If you think you are beaten you are,*
> *If you think you dare not, you don't;*
> *If you'd like to win but think you can't*

It's almost a cinch you won't.

"Life's laurels don't always go
To the stronger or swifter man,
But soon or late the man who wins
Is the fellow who THINKS he can."

—Walter D. Wintle

Why Is This?

You have attended many plays in your life, and the famous player advertised for the star part was always there. "Why is this? Are not actors and actresses human like the rest of us? Don't they get ill like everybody else?" a noted actor was once asked.

"We do not get ill because we cannot afford to. We are advertised to appear. The public expects us. There is no choice about it. We simply MUST go on," he replied.

What Is Like and Dislike?

When we say any one "dislikes" a thing, all we mean is that his *mind is against it.* When he likes a thing, his mind is for it.

Whenever your mind is *for* a thing you can do it, do it well, do it gladly, do it quickly, do it effectively. The doing of it will not tire nor wear you. You will often feel more refreshed at the close of a long day's work at it than you did in the morning 🙠🙠

But when your mind is *against* it you do it slowly, painfully, inefficiently, sadly, and an hour of it leaves you actually worn out physically.

Vocation and Ill Health

For this reason, just so long as you are in work you dislike, you are going to be tired, unhappy, inefficient, nervous, depressed and half sick.

Because the mind builds or bruises the body by every thought it thinks, every negative thought tears down tissue and every positive thought builds it ❧❧

These long-continued negative thoughts are the explanation of ninety per cent of our physical ill health ❧❧

After years of destructive thoughts, the body, which is invisibly interwoven with the brain, is so poisoned it breaks down in its most sensitive spot. What that spot is will depend, in each case, upon the type and temperament of the individual ❧❧

Every physician will tell you that there are sudden breakdowns." When a man unexpectedly goes to pieces" it is "unexpected" only to others. *He* knows there has been something wrong with his mental attitudes for a long while. ❧❧

Where Your Ills Come From

Ninety per cent of your ills do not come from something outside of you as many people imagine, but from something *inside* of you, and that thing is *your mind.* It is a factory manufacturing every moment the things that are going to come out in your life.

You can lead a constructive or destructive existence, just as you choose.

The force that made you, that rules this vast universe, that keeps millions of stars whirling throughout unfathomable space is a constructive force ❧❧

It made the laws, and the laws are no respecters of persons. If you violate the laws you pay the penalty—in illness, failure, death, disease or whatever penalty goes with that particular violation ❧❧

If you obey the laws, place yourself in harmony with these divine constructive forces, and THINK CONSTRUCTIVE thoughts, you will reap the rewards.

Man vs. Savage

The differences between civilized man and the savage; the differences between primitive life and modern life, are differences resulting from man's growing understanding and utilization of these divine laws of the mind. Success for races, nations and individuals is dependent upon a ***working knowledge of law.***

Practical Psychology shows you what these laws are, how to understand their relation to your personal everyday life, and how to apply them to bring you health, happiness and success

The First Step

The first step toward your desires is taken when you realize that YOU make your own happiness or unhappiness and do it by means of your own mental attitudes.

Your mental attitudes are under your control. They may sweep you off your feet for a few moments at a time, but even that is avoidable.

Bulwark yourself with the right fundamental attitudes and nothing can disturb or discourage you

Stop looking around you, outside of you or even above you for the ***cause*** or the ***cure*** of your troubles. The mechanism that brings to pass what happens in your life is ***inside of you.***

Part of the Divine

Man is a part of the universe; he is susceptible to its laws; he invariably reacts to certain conditions in certain ways. Under certain mental conditions he withers, decays. Under certain other mental conditions, he blooms, blossoms and grows. His body is real and knows actual physical pain

But wrapped up within the same being is his spirit—a part of the divine, the ultimate, the force of life itself—as we see from our own aliveness, our own loves and aspirations.

Flesh and Spirit

Where the flesh ends and the spirit begins no one can tell. They are as intricately interwoven as the top branches of two contiguous trees. Whatever helps the mind helps the body, whatever hurts the mind hurts the body.

No man ever kept a healthy body who had an unhealthy mind.

No Use To Move

"You need a change of climate. Go to the seashore or the mountains. Take a trip to Europe," many a doctor has told a patient.

More often than not the patient comes back worse than when he went, and people wonder why. Especially do those people wonder who think how beautiful it would be to take such a trip!

The people who think this would be benefited or not according to what *mental attitudes they took along.*

It, when you pack your grip for a journey you include your Fears, Worries and Anxieties, that trip would do you little good!

But if you will unload from off your back that Knapsack of Fear—thoughts you've been carrying around you won't need a trip!

What Makes Your Environment

"I am stifled by my environment. There is no room here for me to grow," we hear many people say.

Such people believe that certain conditions, individuals, or circumstances in their environment are hindering their progress, happiness, and success. They imagine that so long as these individuals, conditions or circumstances continue in their environment it is useless to try to accomplish anything.

So, they do the one and only thing that is certain to prevent success-stop trying. They reconcile themselves to mediocrity. They get ready to take a half loaf instead of demanding a whole loaf ֍֍

Then when life takes them at their word, they say, "You see I was right. I knew I'd never have any luck."

They do not realize that they got just what they expected, and got it **because** they expected, invited and **manufactured it.**

> *"I bargained with life for a penny*
> *And life would pay no more,*
> *Though I begged so hard at evening*
> *When I counted my scanty store.*
>
> *"For life is a just employer-*
> *It gives you what you ask;*
> *But once you have set the wages,*
> *Why, you must bear the task.*
>
> *"I worked for a menial's hire,*
> *Only to learn, dismayed,*
> *That any price I had asked of life*
> *Life would have paid."*
>
> —Jessie B. Rittenhouse

You Get What You Order

Up to now you have been getting a great many things you didn't want. But you got them because you ordered them yourself.

That you didn't realize you were ordering them doesn't change the facts. You put into operation, because you didn't know any better, the very forces that always bring these undesirable things ❦❦

This course is to show you how to order only *what you want.*

Psychology for All Religions

This course has been compiled in response to a great human need because it is increasingly evident that everyday men and women are becoming very much confused in their attempts to learn the truth about the actual effects of the mind upon the body.

Almost every system of mental healing has, unfortunately, declared that its success came from its connection with some special religious cult, creed or sect, when, as a matter of fact it has come *from the application of psychological laws which are available for every human being who wishes to use them.*

This course is based on eternal principles which operate automatically. These principles are no more dependent upon any particular religious creed than the rising of the sun is dependent upon Methodism, Catholicism or Dowieism.

Psychology Helps Religion

Religion is conducive to health, happiness and achievement but whatever your particular brand of religion the big question is *how well do you live up to it?*

Practical Psychology helps you to live up to your preferred belief, no matter what it is, because it helps you to be happy and healthy; and the happy, healthy man finds it easier to be a *good* man.

It helps you to be true to your religion, regardless of what your religion may be, because it is in accordance with the highest conception of the spiritual in man.

Laws Are for All

The good and great things of life can be had by every person who understands and applies the laws of his own being. These laws are not owned or controlled by any one or by any number of churches, creeds or religions ❧❧

Whether you are a Catholic, a Protestant, a Christian Scientist or a Quaker-or whether you have ever defined your belief by any name at all or not-does not alter the application of these laws to your life. They are for everybody. They are as unchanging as the laws of gravitation, electricity, motion, heat and light.

Like these same laws, they apply to all people, in all countries at all times, under all conditions and civilizations.

To know this all you need to use is your common sense ❧❧

The sun doesn't refuse to shine upon you and shine upon someone else because you don't see religion or the hereafter as he does.

No matter what your religious belief, certain causes will always bring certain results to you. Just so often as you create the condition you will bring the corresponding result, whether you belong to every church or to no church.

Your Life Is in Your Own Hands

No one can live your life for you. No one can make you successful or happy or good or great except yourself. And the only way you can do these things is through your mind, as it expresses itself to the world.

Chance does not rule your life. Accident cannot ruin it. Nothing can hurt you except as you *let* it—and then it is yourself hurting you.

You are the designer of your own future, the contractor and builder of whatever lies in store for you.

It is for you to say what it shall be.

Mind Draws the Plans

Blue prints are the first thing the architect makes when he plans to build. Nothing is done until these drawings are completed.

They contain the plans and specifications. Whatever you have been wishing for and didn't get was somehow left out of your mental blue prints.

Thoughts and Things

Thoughts may or may not be things. But there is no question whatever about thoughts being the *makers* and *producers* of things. They are the self-starters, the forces that cause things to happen; the "power behind the throne" in each of us. "As a man thinketh in his heart so is he."

Tell me how any individual thinks and I will tell you what life is bringing him. Tell me what kinds of thoughts he has habitually entertained, and I will tell you the kind of *life* he has lived.

Tell me what you want to happen in *your* life and I will tell you the kinds of thoughts that help that thing and hinder it—the kinds that make it grow and develop and the kinds that make it decay.

No Secret Thoughts

Every thought you have works for you or against you. There are no "secret thoughts."

They may be concealed for a very short while, but soon they begin to write themselves out for all men to read—in the face, the form, the actions, the *success or the failure* of that person. They publish themselves broadcast for all to understand who study human nature.

Your own thoughts are printed across your brow, in the lines of your face; in the expression and set of your eyes and mouth, and the way you use your hands.

What Are You Thinking?

What you possess today is the *added-up result* of your *old thoughts.*

What you will do or be or have in the future depends on the *kinds of plans* you are drawing for yourself in your private office called "Mental Attitudes."

Ella Wheeler Wilcox, though reared in poverty, became world famous because she believed these things and put them into practice in her life:

> *"That which we call our secret thought*
> *Speeds to the earth's remotest spot,*
> *And leaves its blessings or its woes*
> *Like tracks, behind it as it goes.*
>
> *"It is God's law, remember it*
> *In your still chamber as you sit*
> *With thoughts you would not dare have known*
> *Yet make your comrades when alone.*

"For after you have quite forgot
Or all outgrown some vanished thought,
Back to your life to make its home,
A dove or raven it will come."

What Happens Doesn't Count

"But how can I think pleasant thoughts when so many awful things happen to me?" you say. "How can I be happy?"

You can be happy if you will learn that it is never what happens to you, but how you *take* what happens to you, that counts.

It's not what *comes about*, but what you *think about* it that makes or mars your life.

Your loved ones may die, you may lose your money, you may think you have lost your health, but none of these can permanently ruin your life except as you *allow* them to. And when you allow it *you* are ruining it.

Edmund Vance Cook has said in words that are now immortal—

"Oh a trouble's a ton or a trouble's an ounce,
A trouble is what you make it.
It is not the fact that you're hurt that counts,
But only how did you take it."

How About "Advantages?"

Most people imagine achievement and happiness come from having had "advantages."

Ask any rich man, any successful man, any great man, any famous man what kinds of things in his life had the most to do with his rise.

Will he tell you it was his "advantages?" Will he say it was because everything went smoothly in his life? Will he say it was because he never had any griefs, sorrows, disappointments or delays? Will he say it was due to the fact that he avoided making mistakes?

No! For none of them have been true of any great or successful person. He will say what they all say—"My success? It came from capitalizing my mistakes." All successful people use their disappointments for stepping stones.

Instead of sitting down when trouble comes and making it so comfortable it never wants to leave, such people get up and hustle the thing out of their mental parlors.

Instead of moping and mourning and making everything worse by dwelling on the terrible thing that has happened, they do one little thing that makes all the difference—***renovate their minds!***

Instead of slumping in the dank, dreary basements of depression they live in the sun-parlors on the top floor, something purely ***a matter of choice*** with every human being.

It's Up To You

Whether you live a sad, dejected, despondent, failure-life or a happy, uplifted success-life depends on one thing and one thing only—what you really ***prefer*** to do.

If you don't really ***want*** happiness or only ***wish*** you wanted it: If you get a kind of pleasure out of being wretched or if you "enjoy poor health," you won't get very far. Such a man doesn't try. He likes his misery.

If you ***truly desire*** to be happy and healthy and successful stop wondering this instant whether you can or not. There are actual laws for getting all of them; the laws are in force and have been used, consciously or unconsciously by all who did anything worthwhile in this world.

Power of Thought Known to All

Though men have always recognized the indirect power of thought upon the body it was not until recent years that scientists were able to demonstrate by simple experiments how thoughts react directly upon the physical condition of the thinker.

The most skeptical have been convinced by these manifold proofs, until today every person who has investigated or studied the question knows that thought does vitally, deeply and powerfully affect the bodily processes. They know that good thoughts affect the body favorably, that bad thoughts affect it adversely, and that instead of ill thinking being the result of ill health it is more often the other way around.

Doctors used to say a man was a grouch because he was a dyspeptic. Today they declare he is a dyspeptic because he was a ***grouch first.***

Worry and Cancer

At a recent national convention of leading American physicians, the opinion was expressed that cancer is caused by worry. They declared that in every instance a cancer patient has been a chronic worrier.

In certain types a chronic fear-attitude secretes the poisons resulting in this most dreaded of all diseases. In others it takes the form of various ills, depending upon the type and temperament.

Very brunet, very bony and very mental people are most susceptible to worry.

Worry and Work

Everyone is familiar with the effect of thought upon one's work. He may go through the same muscular performances; he may be on time and work overtime, straining every nerve to live up to his task.

But no piece of work can be done right by muscle alone. The mind must be behind the muscle. The brain must back up the brawn in a man or he will never do anything out of the ordinary ❧❧

Scientific Discoveries

Blood supply and the condition of the blood are, as we all know of the utmost importance to health ❧❧

We also know how our thoughts affect the heart-action and blood supply. All of us are familiar with the paling face of fear, the blushing face of shame, the purple face of anger and a hundred other evidences of how thoughts disturb the blood supply.

Scientists of the highest order have announced their discoveries in the laboratories of the leading universities of this country. Many of these discoveries prove that thought also influences blood supply in more significant ways than we have realized ❧❧

Prof. Elmer Gates of Washington, showed that thinking of any portion of the body causes an increased flow of blood to that part.

The simplest and surest proof of this he demonstrated by placing his hand in a basin in which the water came exactly to the top.

By thinking intently and intensely of the hand as it lay in the water he could cause so great an increase of blood to flow to it that the basin overflowed. With practice any one can do this.

Prof. W. G. Anderson of Yale University proved, by laying a student on a perfectly balanced scale, that the body tipped in the direction of whatever portion of his anatomy the student thought about ❧❧

For instance, the student was asked to think intently of his head. In a few seconds the scale began slowly but certainly to tip downward at the head, showing how the blood had gone to that section in response to concentration.

Then he was told to think of his feet and the scale tipped downward at his feet.

Then he thought of his right hand and it tipped toward the right, but when he thought only of his left hand it swung in that direction.

These are things that all can prove for themselves ❧❧

Sargent, the great physical culture expert of Harvard, proved that mere bodily exercise without proper thought did little to improve health, but that very little exercise would work wonders when accompanied by the right thoughts.

Prof. Jacques Loeb of the University of Chicago, has proved in many ways how thought produces phenomena similar to those of electricity.

He showed how living fiber in the body changes from negative to positive, or from positive to negative accordingly as the individual's thought is negative or positive.

This is perhaps the most significant of all, since science is coming more and more to the theory that man and all other forms of life are expressions of electricity.

That thought effects chemical changes in the body was also proved by Prof. Gates in 1879.

The breath of a patient was held in a tube which had been cooled sufficiently to condense the volatile respiration qualities.

When the patient's mind was at rest no precipitate was observed. It was clear. But within three minutes after the patient became angry there appeared a brownish precipitate. Extreme sorrow produced a gray precipitate. Joy produced a pink precipitate which, when injected into the cells was found to be highly nutritious and to generate energy ❧❧

Illustrations from History

History is full of illustrations of the mind's effect on the body.

Benevento Cellini, one of the greatest sculptors of all time, was taken with a severe illness when just ready to cast his famous statue "Perseus" which is now in Florence in the Loggia dei Lanzi.

He had been in bed for several days. The fever was so high his life had been despaired of, when his friends suddenly rushed in and informed him that the statue was about to be ruined.

"It will be spoiled! The metal is caked. The furnace has hardened it beyond all repair!" they cried ❧❧

Cellini threw on some clothing and ran to the furnace several blocks away.

He had come just in time. Ordering the driest wood, he fired the furnace himself, all the while standing in a drenching rain—but saved the metal.

When it was safe he turned and ate a plate of salad that had been left on a nearby bench, laughed over the victory, shouted with joy and danced around his crew.

Then he recalled that he had been sick, and that it was now two o'clock in the morning.

"But," said Cellini, "I had lost every trace of fever, did not return to my bed at all, and was as well as ever."

Thought also has a decided chemical effect upon the body. This too is a matter of history, as we know upon reading of Marie Antoinette whose hair turned suddenly white during the French Revolution; how Ludwig of Bavaria became snow-white overnight, as did also Charles I of England and the Duke of Brunswick.

Dom Pedro, Emperor of Brazil, who had been lying ill for many months in Europe, was cured instantly by a cablegram from his daughter in which she announced she had just signed a decree for the abolition of slavery in that country, in fulfillment of his lifelong wish.

Elizabeth Barrett had been an invalid all her life. She always lay upon her bed in a darkened room. But when she fell in love with Robert Browning, she flung back the curtains, raised the blinds and was well in an hour!

Thought Power Used Everywhere

That thought has power to help or hinder, to develop or destroy is now so well known that experts in every walk of life are teaching it.

Teachers and preachers have always advocated it, but today the most hard-headed commercial man knows it, uses it hourly in his business, and directs his subordinates to do so.

A Salesmen's Convention

At any salesmen's convention held in the last five years you would have heard much more talk about "mental attitudes" than about "commodities", "commissions" or "territories" though the latter are supposed to be the requisites vital to a salesman's success.

But these most material of modern workers recognize that all success depends on the ***workings of the mind.***

An Advertisers' Convention

Go to an advertisers' convention and you will note that ninety-nine per cent of all the discussions are psychological; that advertising (now the fifth largest industry in America) exists exclusively for and succeeds in exact proportion to its *appeal to the mind.*

A Bankers' Convention

Attend a bankers' convention and note how every speech has its psychological significance. Hear what the leading financiers of America say about minds and how they work; how money affects them; how the lack of money, the borrowing of money, the loaning and investing and the making of money depend on the *mind* of the individual

A Doctors' Convention

That the doctor never cures a patient but only (if he is a good one) gives nature a chance to cure, is now almost as well known to the public as it has always been to the doctors themselves.

The first thing necessary to giving Nature this chance is to remove fear from the patient, and this fact is now being taught in all medical schools

"Make your patient happy and you have started him on the way to recovery," he is told.

Now friend, why go on causing disease and premature death for yourself when you might be building health, wealth and happiness?

Master your thinking and you have mastered your life. Mastering your thinking is easy and simple, once you know how.

Change Your Thought Habits

You have got to change your thinking. To do this is simple when you know the laws of Practical Psychology

The human mind operates in accordance with law. Psychology, "the queen of all the sciences and the science for which all others exist," shows us these laws whereby we make our own lives and how to make what we desire in life instead of what we dread.

But you have got to quit dawdling, dallying and flirting with life. You must stop waiting for "something to turn up."

You can turn up anything you want, but if you sit around and wait the only things that will turn up will be those you do not want.

Elbert Hubbard said, "Everything comes too late for those who only wait."

You would not doubt your ability to train and strengthen your muscles.

Succeeding in life is a matter of training your mind. It is the easiest thing of all to change because its protoplasm is more sensitive, more alive than that of any other part of you, and also because it has an inner urge of its own to express itself constructively.

It is only waiting for you to take off the lid.

Home-Made Hells

The average worrier lives in a hell made by his own thoughts. He could just as easily live in a heaven backed up by facts.

Discouragement is the murderer of achievement. It destroys courage, and we are absolutely dependent upon our courage. Memory, will, initiative—none of them can work without it. We cannot decide unless we have courage; we cannot attempt, branch out nor accomplish anything worthwhile without it.

Yet many worriers never understand why they cannot make their minds work any better, why they have no memory, no power of concentration, no decision. Their minds are clogged with brain ash and clinkers.

Anything you want must be worked out in your own mind before you can work it out in the world. Worry wrecks all your mental machinery.

Living in the Lowlands

Have you not noticed many times in your own life how some great emergency which made a supreme call on you brought out abilities you had not realized you possessed?

Millions of men go through life and into their graves without ever rising to their best selves. They live in the lowlands when they might dwell on the heights. They are sad, dejected and depressed when they might have been happy and truly alive.

They bring old age, decay and death down upon themselves long before their time. Today we say, "He lived to a ripe old age—almost eighty." Some day we will say, "Too bad, he died so young—only a hundred and ten!"

This course places in your hands the knowledge which will enable you to predetermine the content of your consciousness, the condition of your health, the amount of your mental ability and to a great extent, the length of your life 🙚🙚

With its rules you can, if you try—without effort and without strain—live a life that is rich with joy and ripe with achievement.

Your Own Factory

Your mind is like a mighty factory, filled with intricate machinery and run by electricity. It is built to turn out the most wonderful of products—health, success, riches and happiness. You are its master. You can direct its operations and determine the quality and quantity of its output.

But you must furnish it with the right kind of raw materials and learn how to keep the current turned on, or it will do very little for you.

God made the world. But He doesn't make your world. He provides the natural resources. Out of them every man selects what he wants and builds a personal world for himself.

We Build as We Think

We make our own lives, our own success, our own defeat, our own happiness, our own environment—not in an instant but throughout our lives as a whole.

The circumstances of life may place you in an external environment that is foreign to you and your real self. But if you truly want something else you will find it.

Too many people only *think* they want things. They are "wishers" not "willers" nor "wanters." They hold the keys to the very doors of everything they wish for.

But instead of using them they sit on the doorstep crying for someone to open the door and complaining because the door doesn't open itself! ❧❧

What You Will Discover

In this course you will learn, not only how wrong thinking has brought you what you did not want, in the past, but how to make your thinking bring what you do want in future; it will show you how to open the door to the things you desire ❧❧

You will learn how to make every reaction one that shall neither harm you nor anyone else, but shall make you stronger than you were before, *regardless of what happens to you.*

You will learn how to turn poisonous timidity into health-building, wealth-building self-confidence; how to make your mind build your body; how to make every experience a *helpful* experience; how to stop worrying; how to be healthy, young, attractive, efficient and financially independent 🙨🙨

What You Can Do

You can learn how to, so think that an hour of effort brings ten times the results you have been getting out of a week's hard work.

You will learn how to make every moment, and every thought count for you instead of against you; how to think what you wish to think, build what you wish to build into your coming years.

No matter what mistakes you have made, remember, everyone who ever made anything worthwhile in this world made mistakes.

No matter what you have done or have not done:

You CAN be well

You CAN be happy

You CAN be successful

—by following the rules laid down in this course.

It is founded in reliable principles; careful, systematic and accurate observations; laboratory experiments and the most recent scientific discoveries 🙨🙨

Our reason for assuring you that it will enable you to remake your life is that *it has already done so for the authors of this course and thousands of other men and women throughout this country.*

It was first given to the public, through the Benedict lecture courses, published by the present authors, and has been so helpful that new editions are constantly being printed.

"My entire life has been made over by reading your PRACTICAL PSYCHOLOGY course," thousands of letters have said. "I was ill for years but have become well since applying your clear and fascinating laws of health;" and "I was a failure but now I am a success, as a result of your PRACTICAL PSYCHOLOGY course," thousands of others have written.

It can do the same for you.

LESSON I

How To Stop Worrying

"Worry is the cause of more inefficiency, unhappiness and illness than almost any other affliction which modern humanity has to combat. It may well be called 'the disease of the age.'"

—Saleeby

THE rules set forth in this lesson, if faithfully followed, will rid you of the shackles of despondency, fear, doubt and worry. They will free you from the bondage of failure and despair ❦❦

If any of these rules seem too easy or too simple to be adequate, remind yourself that they are scientifically sound.

The psychological processes behind these rules are not simple. They are intricate and complex, just as the scientific processes behind your electric lights are intricate and complex.

But it is not necessary for you to be conversant with the intricacies of electricity in order to light your home. You press a button.

Pressing the Button

In this lesson we are going to show you all you need to know to be free from worry. We shall show you how to press the buttons that will flood your life with brightness. All that is necessary to convince yourself is to try them.

Press the buttons we shall point out to you and see for yourself. The results will amaze you.

A Compact

We are going to make a compact. We will keep our promise and you are going to keep yours.

Our promise is this: We are going to tell you exactly what worry is, what it comes from and how to stop it.

Your promise to us is this: That for the few moments on this lesson you are going to relax, make yourself comfortable in mind and body, listen carefully to what we say and **forget** for these few moments **every problem that troubles you.**

You can do nothing about them for these few moments anyhow. You cannot give your attention to two subjects simultaneously, and for these few moments you are going to give your attention to us ❦❦

After that you may pick them up again and do what you like with them, but for just now you are going to listen to us and let your troubles wait until our little visit is over.

We promise that if you will do this with your whole heart, giving us your **complete co-operation,** relaxing completely and bidding your troubles wait outside the door, you will be able to meet and defeat these troubles and all your future ones.

Worry Tests

Are you a worrier? If you don't know, try these tests on yourself:

Are you in the habit of going over and over and over in your mind the same problem day after day without reaching a conclusion?

Do you take up a fear of misfortune, tragedy, sorrow, hardship or poverty and think about it most of the day

without deciding what to do, and start in next morning all over again? If you do you are a worrier.

Worry vs. Anxiety

Worry is different from other forms of mental disturbance. When you are merely anxious or troubled over a problem you think about it, look on all sides of it, reach a decision and then *do something about it* in accordance with that decision ❧❧

These crucial situations come into the lives of all of us and must be met. All of us lose our loved ones by death. All of us have problems.

In this lesson we do not have reference to these inevitable and temporary crises. They are mental stress in an acute form and must be dealt with as the problem arises, according to the facts of that particular problem. This lesson has reference to a *chronic mental attitude.*

The Chronic Worrier

The worrier seldom realizes his attitude has become chronic; he imagines each day's worry is a separate day's business, not realizing that it is merely a repetition of yesterday's worries and that yesterday's worries were a *repetition* of the worries of last week.

No one likes to admit he is a worrier. We are all convinced that worrying is weakness, but the first step toward curing anything is to confess the fact. ❧❧

Maybe you have been justifying yourself by saying the anxiety you had been feeling was not worry but an attitude necessary to a solution of the problem.

But if the anxiety you are feeling today is centered around the same thing you were anxious about last week or last month or last year, it is just plain worry.

Worry is like a treadmill—you work at it strenuously, but it doesn't get you anywhere. You are in the same spot when you stop as when you started.

What Happiness Is

The happiness of your life is nothing more nor less than the *happiness of your thoughts.*

You have been thinking your happiness or unhappiness was made by the external furniture of your existence—your possessions, your friends, your experiences, the events of your life. We are going to prove to you that this is not so.

Your Mental Pictures

Stop and think of the various places in which you have lived. Some of them were more attractive than others. In some of them you had more property, more of the world's goods than you had in the others.

But if you could choose one of these places and live over again all its experiences, you would not always choose the one in which your material possessions were the greatest, nor necessarily the one in which your physical environment was most gratifying.

You would invariably choose to live over again the months or years in which you had *the happiest thoughts, in which your mind was most at peace.*

That is because your environment is no hard and fast thing. It is not an aggregate of physical realities. Your environment, in so far as it affects your happiness, is composed, not of the actualities, but of a series of mental pictures.

Mind The Real Environment

Your real environment is *within you.* It is not an accidental massing of outward conditions but the product of your own mind.

We have had it borne in on us many times and in many places that it is not your actual surroundings but your thoughts that determine your happiness ༄༄

Psychology of The Prairies

In our travels across the continent, we have shuddered, as we went through the arid western states, at the sight of tumble-down houses whose broken windows, sagging roofs and decayed outlines bespoke a life which to us would be one of unbearable wretchedness.

But we have talked with the women who lived there, and they have told us, while their ragged children clung to their ragged aprons, that they did not mind it. For they did not really live in the hovels with the broken windows. They lived in their thoughts in the hopes of next year's crop and the futures of their children.

Contentment in Chinatown

We have seen the Chinese serenely at peace in their hovels in San Francisco's Chinatown. We have seen contentment and happiness among the poorest immigrants in the tenements of New York's East Side.

Your real environment is inside your head, not your house.

Things and Thinking

Worry is mental auto-intoxication. You are poisoned by yourself.

You veteran worriers have been imagining the source of your worries was in things outside yourselves. This is true only indirectly. The direct cause is your own *fixed attitude.* You relinquish the chair to Fear instead of keeping it yourself.

The events of your life affect your happiness only as they color your thoughts. It is not what happens to you that counts, it is the way you *take* what happens to you. It is never the thing itself that hurts your happiness, it is what you *think* about the thing. Since happiness is a state of mind, we can all see that there is no happiness or unhappiness outside of our own minds.

Your Mental Camera

Every individual makes his own mental pictures. His mind is the moving picture camera that does it. He does it exactly as you take any other kinds of pictures. He turns his mind's eye on certain things just as you turn the lens of the camera on anything when you wish to take a picture of it. If you turn it on pleasant things, it will make you happy. If you turn it on unpleasant ones, it will make you unhappy.

Whether the picture is blurred or distinct will depend, just as in the ordinary camera, on the way you focus it.

Focusing on Fear

Now, with your mental camera, this focus depends on *attention.*

When you close the shutter of your mind's eye till it is focused on just one thing you are giving the concentrated attention which will make it a clear, distinct picture. And it will be filed away in the album of your memory as such.

If your attention wanders—if the shutter is left open so wide that it takes in fringes of the surrounding territory—the picture of the thing itself is less distinct.

What Worry Is

The happiness of any individual begins and ends with these mental pictures. There is no happiness except in the contemplation of these happy pictures. There is no unhappiness save in contemplation of unhappy pictures.

Happiness comes from seeing yourself *as you wish to be.*

Worry is the picturing of yourself *in the situation you fear.*

Turning Your Camera

Let us describe to you what the happy person does. He has given a standing order to his mental photographer not to take any but pleasant pictures.

There are just as many unpleasant subjects within range of his camera as there are within yours, but he ignores them and deliberately turns his on pleasing sights.

The happy man or woman you envy because "they never have any troubles" may have worse ones than yours. If he is an average, self-supporting person it is certain that he has passed through about the same trials, hardships and disappointments you have.

The Three Troubles

Though each case is a slight variation, life is made up of but few different kinds of experiences. Most of the other people in the world have passed through some phases of each of the main human troubles &

There are but four kinds of troubles in the world: Love troubles, health troubles, and money troubles. Four great fears blacken man's life.

They are:

Fear of being unloved.

Fear or being sick.
Fear of being poor.
Fear of being a failure.

Love Troubles

The person who is worried about love turns his mind-camera on the very situation he fears. It is a "movie" camera. It makes moving pictures of him in all the sad situations he can imagine.

Perhaps he has no mate. Like all living creatures, he wants one. Instead of making of himself the happy individual that easily wins love, he devotes much of his time to worrying over his condition. He mentally pictures himself a lonely bachelor. He elongates the picture into the future and sees himself as a lonely, unloved bachelor to the end of his days. He thinks how sad that is going to be, pities himself and dwells on the difficulties of changing the situation. He sees himself growing old with no one really belonging to him and with no one to whom he belongs—*alone in the world.*

He sees himself dining alone, going to the empty home each night through all the coming years. He sees himself craving, but never having, congenial companionship. He sees himself a whitehaired old man with no wife to minister to him and dying with no one to mourn him.

When he visualizes these things day after day, he is doing what all worriers do—sitting in the movie theatre of his mind and running the same reels over and over again.

Your Mental Movie

The duality of every man's nature is clearly shown in this, for you are fully aware that the real you, or ego, sits there in the front row of your mental theatre *watching your other self-acting on the stage.*

Here is another great law of worry. ***Worry tends to bring about the thing you worry about.*** It brings it about because every thought tends to express itself in action.

How Worry Works

When you think of yourself as unloved, lonely, sad and tragic you ACT unloved, lonely, sad and tragic.

No one loves that kind of person. So, the worry about being unloved brings that very condition to pass ❧❧

Perhaps you love someone and are afraid they do not love you. You "worry" about it—make all the pictures for this ten-reel tragedy—and gaze upon them in the secrecy of your soul.

These pictures show you as you imagine you are going to look and feel when you have lost them; you see the humiliated person you are going to be; you see the loved one giving attentions to someone else; you can even see the expression of solicitude in his voice and eyes for that other somebody; you picture yourself heartbroken, desolate ❧❧

This has the same effect on you that worry always has: it makes you ACT OUT in your everyday existence the role you played in these mental pictures—the jealous, heartbroken, desolate one. This makes you unattractive not only to others, but to the very person whose love you wish to have.

"Laugh and the World—"

We all avoid the downcast individual. We have troubles enough of our own. We like to be with the lighthearted folks, because they help us to forget those troubles of ours without loading their own upon us.

The man who worries is the shunned man. That he needs us more than the cheerful man doesn't make up for the unpleasant feelings we get in his company. So we silence the twinges of conscience and stay away from him.

And there is a justice in it after all. For the man who is a drag on his fellows has nothing to contribute to the world.

It is the man who helps to carry the world's burdens who deserves the world's rewards.

The Human Liability

The world owes no man anything, save what he earns, and the chronic worrier whose countenance puts a damper on the cheer of his friends is a liability, not an asset. The result is that inevitably he gets treated as a liability is always treated

Look yourself square in the eye and realize that this is exactly what you are in the eyes of your friends if you are always worrying.

Worry and Friends

Our friends are the gateways through which, directly or indirectly, we get most of what comes to us in life. What they think of us determines the way they treat us.

If we are a worrier people avoid us, and they give us few chances. When we get but few chances to prove ourselves, we are going to get mighty little out of life.

Thus again, our worry indirectly but inexorably brings about what we worry about.

The Why of Poverty

The man of average ability who is poor at forty is usually poor because he has concentrated his best mental energy on the fear of poverty. Eighty per cent of his mind was always fastened, subconsciously, on this fear.

Fear shackles. It crushes. It demoralizes. It chokes the mind and incapacitates it for thinking of the ways and means that would bring money. When only 20 per cent of your mind is given to a project that project won't be much of a success.

Money Troubles

This fear of poverty is the most devastating of these four great fears. It stares the thoughtful man in the face from childhood to old age.

Not knowing the fatal effects of worry he keeps his worry-movie before his eyes every waking moment—a "continuous performance." He watches reel after reel of the distressing pictures—sees himself losing the little he has; sees his struggle to earn more and the failure to get back on his feet; the whole story progresses step by step downward.

In the "final" he gives himself three alternatives—dying in the poorhouse, alone in a garret, or, worst of all, in the home of his uncongenial relatives &‌

Hundreds of our students have confessed that these are the very pictures they visualized for years, in their terror of a "penniless old age."

The Secret of Happiness

You want to learn how to make your imagination work *for* you from now on instead of against you.

You want to be happy instead of unhappy.

Then turn your mental camera on the things you desire instead of the things you fear. In other words, persistently give your ATTENTION to the contemplation of pleasant possibilities instead of unpleasant ones.

Whenever you find that mental camera of yours twisting around toward the things you dread, readjust it till it focuses on the things you want to come true. Then center your attention on them, concentrate on them.

Let your mind dwell on the happy scenes; picture yourself as doing what you want to do, getting what you want. Then you are happy instead of unhappy, optimistic instead of pessimistic ❧❧

Remember, the only thing that makes the happy man different from the unhappy one is that he is CONSTANTLY TURNING THE EYE OF HIS CAMERA ON HAPPY POSSIBILITIES ❧❧

The Happiness Habit

Habit plays a leading part here as in everything we do, and the happy man is helped by habit after he has faithfully turned his camera the right way for a while.

You who have been in the habit of worrying will be hindered by the same law of habit at first, but you can break the bonds of habit by not attempting to break all of them at once.

When you sense the worry feeling coming over you—when the unhappy pictures arise in your mind—don't try to abolish all of them at once ❧❧

You Own the Show

Remember, these worry pictures do not come all at the same instant. They are your enemies, but they cannot come in a mob, for the very simple reason that the mind can give attention only to ONE THING AT A TIME. Each one comes exactly like the separate reels of a movie. You meet these thought-enemies singly.

Because you are bigger than any of your thoughts, you can defeat each one of them as he sticks up his head, *if you want to.*

This is your movie show. You are the owner, proprietor, camera-man and director. You can stop the show any instant and turn on a happy picture.

Remember, the only happiness in life is the happiness you get out of your ***mental images*** just as you make all your unhappiness by your unhappy mental images.

The Convict

Let us take an illustration: To be a convict in prison is considered the greatest tragedy that can befall a man. This man is convicted and sent to prison for twenty-five years. But we don't let him know he is in prison, a branded criminal. We keep these facts from him. We don't let them get into his mind. We convince him that the prison is an institution of honor instead of dishonor, that his friends are proud of him instead of ashamed of him. In short, that it is a distinction to be in prison, that it is the place all of us want to be and all of its phases are delightful phases of existence.

Do you think that man would be unhappy? That he would develop the sad expression, the desolate stoop of the shoulders, the cringing attitude?

Do you think it would ruin his outlook, wreck his life? No indeed. He would be happy every day of the twenty-five years because his BELIEF would be a happy one, his mental pictures would be pleasant ones.

The actual events of his life would be exactly like those of every other convict. The effect on him would be exactly opposite. He would leave there at the end of the twenty-five years a proud, upstanding, courageous man. He would carry his chest up, his head high.

Psychology of Prisons

It is never the fact that a man's body is in prison which hurts him.

The two most famous prison wardens of the United States are Thomas Tynan, head of the Colorado State Penitentiary, and Thomas Mott Osborn, former warden of Sing Sing. Both of these men say it is surprising how quickly the convict adjusts himself to his physical surroundings.

But the thing that kills is what **goes on in his mind**—the **mental pictures of himself** as an outcast ᴥᴥ

So it is with the things that actually happen to you. They cannot hurt you. You hurt yourself, make yourself unhappy because you let them give rise to the wrong kind of mental pictures.

The Citizen

Let us take an opposite case, just to convince you that it is your mental movie and not the facts which make the difference between happiness and unhappiness.

Here is a man who is not a convict. He is, in fact, a highly respected and much beloved citizen of his community.

But by a series of cleverly arranged pretenses we convince him that he has been convicted of crime; we convince him that he is in prison.

Now the place where we are keeping him is not a prison. It is a tall building of beautiful design. But he does not enjoy its beauty. There are flowers everywhere, birds are singing in the nearby trees. There are no bars across the windows, and no lock on the gate. But we convince him that he cannot escape. He believes it.

We allow him to do exactly as he pleases; we let him have family and friends with him precisely as before; we give him everything he asks for.

Do you think he would be happy? With everything tangible that he desired he would be wretched because of his *imagination* that he was a prisoner. His mental images would be unhappy ones—made so, not by the things that happened to him, but by his *interpretation* of them.

And he would leave this beautiful place at the end of even five years a shame-faced, broken man.

When we took him outside and showed him how he could have escaped at any time, that it wasn't a prison at all, we would be doing for him what we want to do in this lesson for you— proving to him that it isn't what happens to you that ruins your happiness; it is whether or not YOU KEEP YOUR MIND ON PLEASANT OR UNPLEASANT PICTURES.

What Thinking Is

If this simile of the mental pictures seems inadequate to you, just remember that your happiness—the supreme aim of life—is all in thinking, and *all thinking is a series of mental pictures.*

If someone else or some force outside yourself made these distressing mental pictures of yours there might be some excuse for your being a worrier.

But *you* make them. You take them, develop them and then watch them unroll before your mind all because you turned your ATTENTION on the wrong scenes.

There are just as many pleasant possibilities in you as in anybody. The external world you live in is the same world the happy man lives in. The same actual stretch or horizon looms ahead of you both. But he focuses his attention on the agreeable and you keep yours on the disagreeable.

Nature on Your Side

And right here let us give you another great law not only of psychology but of biology: Nature is against you when you are focusing on the unhappy scenes; she is on your side whenever you are trying to turn your mental lens on the happy ones.

Why? Because Nature is a constructive force. In fact, "Nature" is the name we have given to the only constructive force we know— the force that makes the grass grow, the flowers bloom, that cures the soldier's gaping wounds, that makes men and women love, that whirls the millions of suns through space.

The worrier is doing a destructive thing, and all Nature opposes him. If he keeps trying, he can make of himself a chronic, self-starting, self-supporting worrier to be sure, but if he can do this with Nature against him, think how much easier he could be a happy man.

Try This

The next time a worry-thought comes sneaking around the door of your mind, instead of flinging it wide open and inviting it in, go to the door and invite in the other guests that constantly hover there—the constructive thoughts, the plans for your future, the things you have to be happy over.

You will be surprised to see how gladly and gratefully they will flock in. They do so because they are your rightful companions, the friends Nature intended you to have.

Something Happens

God never made any creature to be unhappy or unsuccessful. He intended every living thing to be joyous, buoyant, optimistic, and every time we take the slightest step toward them His forces sustain us.

Something happens inside a man the instant he starts striving upward instead of downward—a something that helps him, that strengthens and sustains him ❧❧

When You Are "Blue"

The next time you feel "blue," gently turn your attention to one little happy thought and see what happens to you.

The worrier does the exact opposite. When the happy thoughts come trooping around the door of his mind he ignores them. He keys his mind for Worry's tap, and as if that were not enough stands outside the door looking for her. He welcomes her with open arms, invites the hag into the best parlor and visits with her about all the things he is afraid of.

The sun is shining all around him, the world is a good place, most of the things he fears are not on their way to him at all, and those that are coming will turn out to be blessings in disguise—but he sits there letting Worry blacken the world for him with her insidious threats. Happy thoughts linger around just outside, and one gets near enough to whisper, "Maybe it will come out all right."

Facing "The Worst"

Worry is such a coward that even at this slight whisper she starts to crawl away. But he brings her back, makes her comfortable, and, to justify himself for entertaining her, says, "You see, Worry, you and I have got to get together and look these possibilities all over. To protect myself against the worst, I must *know what the very worst could be*, so you just go on. Tell me every awful thing that might happen to me. Describe the details to me. Don't withhold anything." ᏕᏖᏕᏖ

And Worry, loathsome scandal-monger that she is, whispers back, "Well, here are some of the deplorable things that may come,"—and goes on as long as you will give her your attention, picturing to you the terrible tragedies that are possible ᏕᏖᏕᏖ

Worry A Liar

You let yourself believe her. To be sure, you know that Worry is a liar. You recall that nine tenths of the awful things she predicted in the past never came true. You begrudge the time you wasted listening to her before. You realize all too well if you had used that time to do something worth while you would be *far ahead of where you are today.* You despise her for the harm she has done you. You have nothing but contempt for her. You wish she would stay away from you. You wish you never had to see her disgusting face again. ***And you don't have to, if you don't want to*** ᏕᏖᏕᏖ

Worry A Coward

But Worry is like a human being. She gravitates back to the place where she is welcomed, and when you are so kind to her, and give her so much attention, she hangs around.

She is also like humans in this: she stays away from the places where she is not welcomed. Only she is such a cowardly, cringing thing she is much more easily rebuffed than a human being. One lifting of your chest and she vanishes. Straighten your shoulders, raise your head, and she is gone.

To be sure, she doesn't go far away. She watches for the flash to die out of your eye, the droop to come back to your shoulders, for she knows what these mean in your mental attitude. She knows the stooped man is her prey.

Chests and Courage

All thoughts have their physiological expression, and one always induces the other. The sunken chest is the mate of Discouragement. The lifted chest is the mate of Courage. They are like two animals in the jungle: when you see one you know the other is not far away.

So, when Worry sees your head high, she slinks farther away. Try it and see.

The Wrong Way

Don't continue to labor under the delusion that it is hard to stop worrying. You make hard work of it because you go at it wrong.

You try to slay all of your enemies at once. You forget that the only enemies to your happiness are your thoughts and you cannot have two opposite thoughts simultaneously.

All you need to do to get rid of Worry is to let another visitor in.

The minute you open the door of your mind to the courageous thoughts that hover there, Worry wraps her rags about her and slinks out. You don't need to order her to go. Don't dignify her that much.

Don't recognize Worry as worthy of your consideration. She is nothing but a ***black Nothingness*** created by the weak side of your own mind anyhow. ***She has no existence save as you create and recreate her.***

"Hope Springs Eternal"

Never be afraid that the good thoughts aren't just outside the door.

What is it that keeps every living creature battling hopefully to the last minute of life, sustains the sick, the decrepit, the defeated, and lures them to fight on? It is these encouraging thought-friends. They are always there, re-assuring you, whispering hope into your ear whenever you stop gossiping with Worry long enough to listen ❧❧

Thought-Qualities

In this lesson we do not ask you to tackle Worry and forcibly eject her. That is not necessary. Open the door of your mind to the tiniest constructive thought and before you can see what is happening, Worry dodges away.

This is due to a psychological law and the law is that ***thoughts are accompanied by emotional qualities or tone.*** Every thought you have gives rise to a definite, though sometimes imperceptible, reaction ❧❧

Whenever thoughts of achievement, health, love or prosperity cross your mind you experience a feeling of courage, energy and stimulation.

Whenever ideas of death, disease or failure flit across your mind you experience instantaneously a feeling of lethargy, inertia and impotence. Sad memories, remorse or fear have associated with them disintegrating emotional qualities.

Exalted ideas, inspiring hopes have associated with them energizing and vitalizing emotional qualities. Such is the miraculous mechanism of the human mind.

Images and Emotions

As we have seen, all happiness or unhappiness comes from your mental pictures. They come because your mental pictures are each mated to an emotion.

Unhappiness is the massed emotion from a series of unhappy pictures. Your mind-camera is taking pictures for you every waking moment, and just as long as you turn it on unpleasant thoughts you will have unhappy emotions or worry

Push The Clock Ahead

Worry comes from exaggerating the importance of ourselves. It is a big universe. What happens to you and me doesn't make such a lot of difference after all. Even to you and me it doesn't make much difference.

Think where you will be a hundred years from today. Think where you will be one year from today. A year from today you will say today's worries were wrong, useless, demoralizing.

Knowing this is what you will say about them only a year hence, why not push your imaginary clock a year ahead and say it now?

Give today to something constructive. Give it to something which you can be proud of a year from today.

Captain Stormfield

When you find yourself taking yourself and your little life too seriously, turn to that famous story of "Captain Stormfield's Visit to Heaven," which Mark Twain wrote. For fear you can't get it in a hurry when you need it, we will give you the gist of it here.

The Captain found great difficulty in making clear to the angel at the gate just who he was. He was sure St. Peter would remember him as soon as he mentioned his name. He greeted him familiarly and announced he was Captain Stormfield.

St. Peter didn't seem to know of any such man. Then he explained that he came from San Francisco. Nobody in heaven had heard of San Francisco. Then he told them that San Francisco was in California. That meant nothing, so he informed them that California was in the United States. The United States, he said, was in America. Nobody had ever heard of America.

At last, he told them he came from the Earth. After a long search through the archives, someone discovered a slight reference to a speck, out among the billions and billions of stars, planets and constellations, called the Earth.

A Big Show

The marvels of time are as wonderful as the marvels of space. This is a Big Show. Nobody knows how many billions of centuries it has been running, where it started or where it is going.

We are infinitesimal atoms. If the worst thing that could happen to an atom happened to us it wouldn't be very important. About the only thing we can do to prevent being even more insignificant is to be as constructive as we can. To do this you must remove worry, the most destructive attitude, from your mind.

Failure Worries

If you worry about failure, just remember that nothing will bring failure so surely as that fear. Your place in life today is the massed result of the ***thoughts of your yesterdays***. Your life is made, to an astounding degree, by your thinking.

If you would realize success tomorrow, think success today.

No chronic worrier ever achieved success. You know why. Your success in this highly organized social structure depends to a great extent on other people. What other people think of you determines the chances to be offered to you this coming year. If you are a worrier, they know it. Nobody dares trust a worrier.

The Ingrowing Mind

It takes clear concentration to accomplish anything. The worrier can't concentrate on his work because most of his attention is concentrated on himself —turned inward on his petty personal concerns. If you worry about ill health, you start ill health.

Your worry thoughts create toxins which, as you have seen in the preceding pages, poison the entire system.

Worry and Disease

Your body and mind are closely related. No worrier can stay well. The man with a sick mind soon has a sick body. His worry is a factory that works overtime ***manufacturing disease.***

If you are one of those who have a vague fear of what the future may bring; of what may "happen to befall," remember that you, not chance, are the architect of your future. You are building toward it today and the plans and specifications are all drawn by your mind.

Plans and Specifications

If you are keeping your mind busy drawing pictures of the things you dread, you are not only giving it no time to plan constructively but are allowing it to make the very outlines you don't want to follow.

Every thought tends to express itself in action. THIS IS A FUNDAMENTAL PSYCHOLOGICAL LAW. You can't think one way and act another; you can't think failure and build success ❧❧

Meet Today Now

If you worry over your past, you are like a certain type of the insane. All asylums are acquainted with the inmate who sits rehearsing the events of his past and refuses even to dress himself for the day.

If you are concentrating on unhappy memories, you are refusing to meet today. If you are permitting grief, remorse, bitterness or regret to absorb the very source of your creative powers—your mind—you are ***committing mild suicide***.

Tomorrow this day will be a part of your past. If you waste it, you add the regret of having wasted it to the long list of regrets you already have.

If you would lessen tomorrow's remorse, make today constructive.

Bury Your Past

Bury your past and don't visit the grave. If you did things or failed to do things that hurt you in the past, don't let them stretch their slimy hands into your future and ruin that also.

The past is gone. It will never return. You knew this before we told you. The idea is not original with us.

If you will thrust your past out of your consciousness whenever it raises its accusing head, it can do you no harm. It can only harm you as you give it your ATTENTION. Transfer your attention to other things whenever it approaches and eventually it will return no more.

Digging Up Dead Fears

No matter what you have done or left undone it is over and done with. If you did wrong, you are making it worse by burning the incense of memory at its altar. If you committed a sin, you are dyeing it deeper every time you honor it with your thoughts, for your ***thoughts make it live again*** and nothing else can.

If it was a real sin, the only atonement you can make is to devote your attention to its opposite now. If you think about it you are incapable of doing its opposite for our actions follow our thoughts. The man who worries over his past sins is piling up sins in today.

Keep Your Chest Up!

No matter what you have done, no matter of what crime you may be guilty, raise your chest, lift your head, look the world in the eye.

We want you to do this because these are the first steps toward accomplishing anything great.

If you have done wrong in the past you want to make up for it in the future. You can't do anything to make up for it if you go around with your head hanging.

No human being has a right to ask you to hang your head, anyhow. All human beings are pretty much alike. All of us are big bundles of instincts. Crime is the over-indulgence in certain instincts ♦♦

With the same instincts equally developed and the temptation equally great, the people who are criticizing you would doubtless have done just as you did—maybe worse.

Respect Yourself!

Stop despising yourself. God made you. He gave you the instincts. He knows your temptations. He knows that every human being does the best he can under every given circumstance, with the nature he has—not necessarily the best he knows, but the very best the combination of his particular instincts plus his particular temptation permitted of at the time.

Don't let anyone tell you that God likes to see you ashamed, stricken, crushed to earth. That is man's poor little mean way—the craving to see those who disobey him humiliated.

The Force that rules the universe, that keeps myriads of worlds operating with divine accuracy throughout unfathomable space, must be a constructive Power. The only sure way to worship it is not in self-abasement but in self-mastery.

Your Face to The Sun

The bigger your sin the greater the need for your doing something splendid today. No man ever did anything splendid whose head hung in shame. Lift yours to the sun. It will tell you more about the real God than all the human beings can tell you in a thousand years.

It will tell you that everything from sunflowers to human beings must keep their faces upturned ***toward the light***, if they would grow.

Don't Walk Backward

You have a future to build. The more regrettable your past, the more necessary is it that you build a shining, worth-while future. You can't build anything worth-while with your eyes on the past.

What would you think of an auto driver who tried to steer his car up a rocky grade with his eyes on the road behind him instead of the road ahead? What if he kept looking at all the crooked tracks he had made back there and scolding himself for them?

What if he said over and over, "Oh, what a mistake that was! I should have known better! That was a blunder, over there was another and away back there several miles I nearly ran into the ditch!" Perhaps he actually had a blow-out or a wreck somewhere back there.

Would you expect anything like expert driving from that man if he kept worrying about that wreck? No, indeed. You would tell him to forget the crooked tracks, the narrow escapes. Yes, and the wreck, too.

Nobody is going to take the trouble to trace the windings of your route.

Don't Worry Over Gossip

It isn't as popular today to be a self-constituted detective as it used to be. Human bloodhounds no longer have standing even in the church.

The man or woman who today takes it upon himself to pry into the poor, unhappy past of another struggling human atom is no longer credited with virtuous motives. We know him for just what he is—*a scavenger*.

The man who tells anything derogatory to another human being is telling a *much worse* story on himself. He is telling that he has a putrefied mind 🙠🙠

Your Own Optician

Each of us sees the world through our own spectacles. Keeping rosy glasses before your eyes makes the world a beautiful place. Wearing dark ones will not make the world dark, but it will make it dark FOR YOU.

If you have a habit of seeing evil in others it is because you have evil in you. For we not only wear our own glasses, we *make* our own glasses out of our minds.

Steer Straight!

You are driving the car of your life up the arduous grade of the future. Every time you look behind you, you are missing the best places in the road of today. That means more crooked tracks for you to regret tomorrow.

If you don't want all the Tomorrows filled with regrets for Today's poor driving, forget the poor driving of Yesterday and steer the best you can from this point onward.

All Alike

The tracks you have made, bad as they may have been, are not very different from those of your fellow travelers, after all. We are all surprisingly alike. Kipling expressed it when he said, "The Colonel's lady and Judy O'Grady are sisters under the skin." Alice Duer Miller had Life's roadway in mind when she said,

"Democracy is this:
To hold that all who wander down the pike
In car or cart, on foot or bike,
Are much alike, are much alike."

You may be riding up this highway of life on the bicycle of a 20-dollar-a-week job; you may be ambling along in a 10-dollar-a-week cart, but don't let these things humiliate you.

There is mighty little difference between you and the man who skims past you in the big limousine. Realize this fully and you will have taken the first step toward a limousine of your own 👁👁

The Salve of Envy

Don't spend your precious time envying the other fellow near you on the road. Don't salve your wounds with the notion that he stole his limousine or got a "head start." These things have been done but those who do them don't last. They fall behind in the race.

It isn't the "start" found in the money some people inherit. The man who inherits a "head start" isn't as well equipped as the one who reaches the same place by his own efforts.

When the race ends it is the men who have struggled every inch of the way that *come in first.*

Life's Relay

The thing that counts is your driving. It's the way you steer and handle your "bike" that wins you a Ford or a limousine farther up the hill.

Life is a relay race. You change to a faster vehicle as soon as you have earned it. The road is lined with all kinds of cars. The kind you will have next year depends on the efficiency of this year's driving, and the amount of excess baggage you have in your load.

All regrets, remorse and despair over Yesterday are so much excess baggage. Get rid of them.

In the famous Marathon races of ancient times the runners stripped themselves of everything that could in any way hinder freedom of movement or impede their progress.

Strip for The Race

Rid yourself of everything that handicaps your efforts. Let go of everything that shackles you. Strip clean for the big race. Unload from your car every ounce of chagrin and self-depreciation. "Travel light" as the globe trotters say.

Then to win, keep your hand on the wheel, your eye on the road ahead and don't let any one pass you in your own make of car.

Learn from Your Mistakes

You are going to dump out of your car today the load of sadness, sorrow and regret you have been carrying. As you throw each package away take a good look at it and find what there was in it that *taught* you something.

Every unhappy experience you ever had concealed a lesson in it somewhere. If you don't know where, scrutinize it till you find it.

We do not maintain that all your troubles are sent by a benign Providence as blessings in disguise. Most of your troubles are the result of your having *violated natural law.*

But we do know that you can sift out of each tragedy a grain or two of knowledge that will protect you in the future.

"Capitalized Failures"

It often happens that the tragedy it prevents would have been worse than the one you had. Many a man has said that his success was built on the knowledge gained from his failures. One of America's most successful men said recently:

"My success is my failures capitalized. I cashed in on my mistakes.

"I made some of the worst ones; the number and variety of my blunders, sins and failures was alarming. And how I worried about them! I dragged around with me more dead weight of depression than any one I knew.

"It is a long story, how I changed my life, but it can all be told in this: I determined to cast off every form of fear. I did it by turning my attention away from past failures and concentrating it on ways and means for profiting by those failures. Today I have those old tragedies to thank for my happiness and achievement."

Live In the Now

One of the best antidotes for "past" and "future" worries is to let yourself live more in the "now." Live today within today. After all, the only living you ever do is what you do in the eternal Now ❧❧

Man crucifies himself between two thieves. On one side is the thief of the Past, a dark-visaged spectra of lost opportunities, blasted hopes, blighted ambitions. On the other is the Future—glowing, rosy, radiant with the things we hope to achieve—but in reality, as dangerous a thief as the other, for he deters you from effort with his false promises. He justifies your neglected tasks, your wasted hours and slipshod ways by saying, "I am going to make up for it in the future."

That lying, luring phantom—the phantom of a Tomorrow that is never here—steals your life ❧❧

Todays and Tomorrows

Remember, Today is all you have. Yesterday is gone forever and Tomorrow will never come.

Everything that was ever done was done in the glorious living Todays. Today you are alive. Today is here. Today is yours. You can use it or throw it away.

The difference between those who achieve and those who fail is that the achieving ones value their Todays.

Life's Little Worries

"I saw something once that graphically impressed this upon my mind.

"I was on a train going to keep a Chautauqua engagement. At a small station an old lady and her son got on and took the section opposite me.

"The mother had brought so many bundles there was no room for the son, so he came over and sat with me.

"He explained that this was his mother's first railroad journey. She was very old and disliked the idea of going away from her own home even to visit relatives.

"But they had at last induced her to take this little trip of twenty miles to Springfield where her other son lived. She was as excited as a child and had looked forward with the greatest anticipation to the journey.

"But she had insisted on bringing with her as many of her belongings as both of them could carry. She was almost submerged under the piles of bundles, grips, suitcases, packages, bird cages and boxes, and these she kept rearranging, changing and fussing over.

"Her son, who wanted her to see all the interesting things along the way, would lean over every few moments and say, 'Look, Mother,' but the old lady, without turning away from her packages, answered, 'Yes, son, just as soon as I get these things fixed the way I want them.'

"It was a pretty stretch of country in a New England state. Low hills, carpeted with fresh spring grass, rolled away to the eastward. We saw a meadowlark here and there. But the old lady was too intent on her belongings to look up.

"After a while, just as she seemed to have the last box stowed away and everything adjusted to suit her, the conductor came down the aisle calling, 'Springfield—all—off—for—Springfield,' and at his heels the porter, reaching for the old lady's bundles.

"I shall never forget the dismayed look on her face, 'You don't mean this is where I get off! Oh, I just got my things fixed ready to enjoy the scenery! Surely, it's a mistake. This can't be our station' ⛺⛺

"The porter assured her it was and hustled her and her possessions out on to the platform."

Life on the Limited

There are lots of people like that old lady. Maybe you are. You are always getting ready to live, preparing to enjoy life. You are spending all your thought on the petty concerns of today— the little bundles of daily worries—with never an outward gaze toward the beauties on the horizon.

And some day, just as you get the poor little affairs adjusted ready to sit back and live the Conductor will call your station; the black porter, Death, will turn deaf ears to your wails and hustle you off the car. The world will go on without you.

Today you are still on that train. It is flying faster than the Twentieth Century Limited, which makes the trip between New York and Chicago in eighteen hours.

Every day, every hour you are passing through a wonderful country, which you will have no chance to see again.

Life is a one-way journey on a limited—no round trips and no stops.

If you want to make the most of it, arrange your baggage by organizing yourself efficiently. Then take time to enjoy the journey.

One Minute at a Time

No man ever sank under the burdens of today. It is only when we add to Today's burdens the memory of Yesterday's and the imagination of Tomorrow's that the load seems more than we can bear ❧❧

You are called upon to live only *one minute at a time.* Control your thinking minute by minute and you have solved the worry problem.

The usual way people set about stopping worry is a wrong one. That is why it is so unsuccessful. The worrier tries to cure himself by the sheer power of his will. This is a mistake.

Worry is never to be beaten by force. YOU HAVE GOT TO REPLACE IT WITH SOMETHING ELSE.

Be Patient but Persistent

When your mind gets to dwelling upon someone troublesome matter with feverish insistence, when you find yourself irritable, depressed, over wrought, gently *turn your attention* to something else ❧❧

At first you will be troubled by your mind slipping off the thoughts. Bring it back each time, not with a jerk, not with force, but quietly, patiently. Do this each time and after a few times it will stop trying to wander.

This is not only the secret of conquering worry but of developing the most valuable of all mental faculties—concentration.

Attention The Secret

Your attention is what determines your happiness. You control your attention. You are its master. You can, at any moment, take it away from one thing and place it on another. Unless you are feeble-minded you can do this, and we know you are not feeble-minded because no feeble-minded person would be reading this course.

You cannot kill worry by blows or any kind of direct fighting. You can't kill it by simply saying, "I am not going to worry."

Turn on the Light

If you went into a dark room and wanted it light you would not try shoveling out the darkness, would you? You would turn on the light.

Worry is a mental darkness. Picks and shovels won't remove it, but turning on the light will.

Here is another natural law: No two things can occupy the same space at the same time. No two thoughts can occupy your mind at the same time.

Whenever you want to be rid of a worry thought, deliberately turn on the light by turning to a pleasant thought. You can think only one thing at a time and if you think courage or joy you can't think worry thoughts at the same time &⏳&

Control Your Attention

The cure is for you to make by constantly switching your attention from the sad to the glad spots in your environment. We are only the messengers of truth, the purveyors of this knowledge. No one can make you stop worrying. We are showing you in this lesson just how you can cure yourself &⏳&

The foundation upon which this lesson is based is the great law that *no two objects can occupy the same space at the same time.* We repeat it here for it is the most important thing in this lesson.

When worry is occupying your attention, all good thoughts are shut out. When confidence is in possession, worry is out. That is all there is to the law of worry—a big law but simple to operate, just as the greatest machinery is operated by the pressing of a button.

Earn Your Happiness

The fact is that the real responsibility rests upon **you**. And that is just, for the man who wouldn't brace up enough to apply these simple rules hasn't *earned* peace of mind.

Whether or not you are worth saving is somewhat determined by whether or not you have the little bit of backbone necessary to follow these few rules in your daily life.

Worry An Unreality

Start today with the fixed conviction that worry is a mental condition; that it is unreal and like all unreal things can not hurt you unless you are afraid, and even then it is only your own *fear* that hurts you.

Worry may make horrible pictures in your mind; she may distort and magnify your problems. But if you will put a little starch into your jawbone and your backbone you can expel her instantly.

She may come back, that is true. But if you can throw her out once you can again. You can't cut down a tree with one blow of the axe. But many blows and it falls for good.

Weed Your Garden!

Your brain is a garden. In it there are roses and weeds fighting for possession. If you let the weeds get ahead the roses will die. But if you will snip off the weeds as fast as they appear above the ground, the roses will thrive.

You must be vigilant. You must nip your bad thoughts in the bud. Whenever a worry weed pops up in your mental garden, call on your will power for its scissors. Say to yourself, "This thing is negative, unreal; it is a bugaboo, a black nothingness. And I, a human being, a living, thinking creature, am not going to be downed by a thing that exists only in my own imagination.

You are free. You have your place in the world. You, and nothing else, are master of your thoughts. You have enough will power at this moment to carry you through, and you are going to have more when you have read the rest of this course.

"Fear no evil." The worst evil that can befall you is worry and you can forestall that. The weeds in your brain garden will die of neglect if you give your attention to nourishing the flowers.

Breathing vs. "The Blues"

The next time things are discouraging to you, instead of weeping at the shrine of Fear, try this: At first, if it seems hard to smile or transfer your thoughts, walk to your open window; raise your chest; lift your head and breathe deeply for just two minutes. You will be amazed to see what happens to you. You are not as worried as you were two minutes before.

No one can be desolate when his lungs are full of good fresh air. All worry has a physical aspect and when your lungs are full of good air all your physical processes are vitalized.

If air were something only millionaires could get there would be some excuse for you. But it is the freest thing in the world. It is our greatest necessity and Nature put it everywhere for us. One good lungful of it and you are a changed man.

Survival of the Strong

Nature is your friend, the guardian angel that hovers over you every moment, ready to help you the instant you will let her. For Nature, you know, has her big purpose of life-preservation in view, and the weakling thwarts that purpose. The moment you start being strong she puts her forces behind you. If you keep trying she will see that you don't fail.

Hereafter, when worry thoughts creep in, when depressing mental pictures begin to get hold of you, take the deep breaths that start your blood racing. This gives you pleasanter thoughts, for the simple, scientific reason that no brain can have "the blues" when the blood is circulating rapidly through it.

Throwing The Switch

Depression is always associated with sluggish physical processes and especially with lazy blood circulation. Every deep breath speeds up heart action and thus stirs the whole circulatory system to keener activity.

But don't stop at deep breathing. Turn on the current of your mind. Let happy thoughts assume vividness in your mind; talk to someone whose presence reassures you; listen to cheerful music; read a story, a magazine article or a Walt Mason jingle—anything to throw the switch on your train of thought and send it down another track ༺༻

Don't Cheat Yourself

There are hundreds of things you can do to send your thoughts into pleasant channels if you try. The trouble with the chronic worrier is that he won't try. He says, "I'll try it, but *it won't do me any good.*" Of course it doesn't. For he hasn't really tried. When you start with a negative attitude you are not trying.

Worry, like Memory and Will, is a mental thing. These are somewhat like human servants. They don't do a thing if they know you are not expecting them to.

Breaking Your Maverick

Your mind is an unbroken colt, a maverick. It rebels against training at first, but pretty soon, if you keep the reins in your hand and follow these rules, it will be the servant of your will. You can guide it wherever you wish. You can guide it into the habit of right thinking, optimistic thinking, constructive thinking. *The man who has mastered his thinking has mastered his life.*

Think Well of Yourself

If people only knew what they are doing when they allow themselves to think they are failures, when they picture themselves as nobodies!

If they could only see how these images of weakness etch themselves into their brains, usurp the reins and take charge of their affairs, nothing could induce them to harbor them for an instant. They would drive them out as they would expel a robber from their homes.

Letting the Thieves In

We carefully lock the door of our offices and homes against thieves but leave the doors of our minds open to the thieves of worry that rob us of happiness, health and efficiency.

No matter how priceless may be the valuables in your office or home, the loss of them all would be nothing compared to the loss of hope, courage and confidence.

Your success depends, not on any of the material belongings you may have locked up in the safe, but on *the state of your mind from day to day* ❦❦

Get Away from Fear

Fear is the worst enemy you have. It is the only enemy that can down you. It can only do so if you let it. It is powerless to harm you except as you bow down to it and relinquish yourself into its hands.

What would you think of a man who persisted in keeping his bitterest enemy near him all the time? You would say he was a fool.

This is exactly what the chronic worrier does. If Worry wanders away for a moment, Habit runs after her, brings her back and the worrier gives her his attention. As we have pointed out before, the thing that has your attention has the richest gift you can bestow.

Forget Your Enemies

It is for this same reason that we don't want you to worry over any of your human enemies. Many people worry because they have been wronged. Doubtless people have wronged you.

Everyone has been wronged, mistreated, misjudged, misunderstood. Anyone who ever did anything worth doing has been misunderstood. Anyone who ever mingled much with others has been hurt sometimes in the shuffle.

But that is all the more reason why you should not let people hurt you anymore.

When you worry about the wrongs done to you, you are laying at the feet of those who hurt you the most precious gift you can give-your thoughts. Now if he wronged you unintentionally you have no right to judge him. If he wronged you intentionally that man certainly does not deserve these priceless gifts of yours. The only way to vanquish an enemy is to grow so big you *forget him.*

Don't Show Sensitiveness

If you are inclined to be sensitive to what people say about you, to worry over what people may think of you, there is just one way to silence them. Moreover, it will make them admire you. That is never to let them know you are sensitive.

The "survival of the fittest" is an unwritten law that has almost as much power in the human world as in the animal, and everyone knows what occurs in the animal world when a creature shows fear.

Did you ever notice what happens to the dog that goes around with his tail between his legs? Every little terrier snaps at him. He is usually a rather nice dog, just as sensitive people are often higher, evolutionally, than those whose criticisms they fear. But they will never go far till they school themselves to ignore the carpers.

Let Them Talk!

Elbert Hubbard said, "There is only one way to ward off criticism: be nothing, say nothing, do nothing." &&

Anyone who accomplishes has mud spattered on him occasionally. If you want to escape with the minimum of mud let people know their mud neither interests nor harms you.

The world does homage to the man who *isn't afraid of it.* It snaps at the one who is always on the lookout for its opinion.

Never worry over what people are saying about you and they will never say anything very bad &&

On the other hand, the man who is always worrying about what the world says of him will never give it reason to say anything very good.

Your Mental Power House

If you had a big manufacturing plant run by electricity, do you think you would leave the power house, where all the current was generated, wide open to thieves and vandals? Do you think you would go so far as to encourage them to come in and pilfer? Would you keep your most valuable servant, Attention, stationed at the door to welcome them in to destroy?

You would not think of doing such a thing. You would keep that power house guarded day and night, you would let no one into it who would harm the priceless machinery, and you would employ in it only the most efficient assistants ❖❖

Your mind is your power house—the station that generates the current by which everything you do in life must be accomplished. Worry, fear, anxiety and doubt are the vandals that wreck its delicate mechanisms.

Yet you worriers let them plunder around in there at will, sapping your vitality, destroying your initiative, demoralizing your greatest forces.

And not this alone: These thieves turn the current of your power against you and burn down your property.

Many diseases and most failures are the direct results of this great power being turned against you. Learn to lock them out. Refuse them your attention and they are helpless to harm you.

Your Movie Tragedies

If you have followed us closely up to this Point you now realize that all worry is merely *a series of unpleasant mental pictures*; that when you sit in the movie theatre of your imagination, gazing at those unpleasant pictures over and over again, you are worrying.

As we have pointed out, these pictures are made by the turning of your attention on the unhappy subject. We have shown you that all you need to do to free yourself of worry is to turn your attention to a ***happy subject*** in your life ♪♪

To do this, let the happy subject assume ***greater vividness*** than the other and then hold it there. This is the secret of attention. This can be done for a few seconds at a time by any one of average intelligence.

And when you have done it for a few seconds at a time you can soon do it for a few moments at a time. Soon you will be able to sustain this happy mental attitude over a period of half an hour, then an hour and gradually to whole days.

Snub Madam Worry

"Be free of worry for days at a time?" you ask. Certainly. To be sure, Worry will come near the door of your mind often at first, for you see, she has the habit because you have been so good to her ♪♪

But when you ignore her and give your attention to uplifting thoughts she acquires another habit—the habit of tapping on your door less often. After a little while she will come only occasionally, and then there will come the time when she troubles you only at wide intervals.

Automatic Attention on Happiness

By that time you will have mastered your mind so well that your subconscious will turns her away without interrupting you. You will be so completely the ruler of your life that you will scarcely be aware of her presence.

Start today. When you fail don't be discouraged. Try again. Remember the happiness of your life depends on the happiness of your own thoughts and you make your thoughts by the placing of your attention.

You are a free agent. You are the captain of your own mental ship. You can pilot it wherever you will. You can think the thoughts that are agreeable to you. You can, at any moment, produce in consciousness uplifting, inspiring thoughts. By so doing you can build an uplifting, inspiring life.

Thoughts That Work for You

You are going to start right now to build the kind of future you want. You are going to set your great forces working for you instead of against you. You are going to devote your mind to drawing the kind of plans you want to come true instead of the ones you dread/You are going to right about face and start up the road to Success regardless of what anybody thinks or says. You are going to apply these simple, easy rules and remake your existence into a happy, healthful, joyous life.

Don't Tell Everything

Let us give you a parting secret—a secret which is "just between you and me." Don't explain your plans, don't announce your new regime to anyone. Soon they will be wanting to know what has made the beautiful change in you. Then will be the time to tell them, and to pass this lesson on so it can help them as it has helped thousands of others.

LESSON II

How To Be Self-Confident

"It matters not how strait the gate,
How charged with punishments the scroll,
I am the master of my fate;
I am the captain of my soul."

—William Henley

HAVE you ever gone into a situation with all the materials for winning and lost just because you *lacked self-confidence?* ::

Have you ever been tortured by the humiliating knowledge that due to your self-consciousness you had cut a sorry figure before one whom you especially wished to impress?

Have you stayed awake nights imagining how much more creditably you could acquit yourself if you could only try it over again? Have you made plans for retrieving your lost ground with that person and invented ways and means of meeting him again to show him your strong, true self?

What Self-Confidence Does

These things have happened to millions of people. Countless men and women of brilliant qualities suffer humiliation, despair and failure merely for the lack of self-confidence, while others of less ability walk off with the world's prizes because they possess this quality.

High places are full of mediocre individuals who got there almost solely on their self-confidence. Many a superior soul has gravitated to a lowly station and been compelled to stay there solely because he lacked it.

Your Front Windows

Perhaps someday the fairy tale we were taught at school, to the effect that "merit always wins" may come true, but nothing could be further from the truth today.

Today the world is organized of the self-confident, by the self-confident and for the self-confident.

The standard by which the world measures is not "How much pure gold is there in you?" but "How much brass have you mixed with it?"

To be sure, you must have real gold in you. If you haven't, the acid tests of competition will soon show it and you will be thrown out on the dump ಬಿಡು

But gold alone won't do. Everywhere the demand is for the individuals who have not only a good stock of goods, but whose "front windows" show to advantage. You are well acquainted with this in the business and professional world.

Self-Confidence and Love

But it is getting to be true also in the realm of romance. The girl who was modest, self-depreciatory—the kind they said had a heart of gold"—used to be the kind men wanted to marry.

But the modern man knows that kind of girl won't make the showing he needs. So, he marries the girl with snap and self-confidence.

And you can't blame him. A man's wife must be a helpmate today just as always. She must be an asset. She must, just as always, meet his friends, associates and superiors with the manner betokening his success.

Self-depreciatory, self-conscious people can't do this. Less confidence is had in you the minute you are known to be allied with timid people.

In the good old days when a man's wife was considered somewhat as a bit of his personal was property that modest, shrinking manner fine. Naturally, one didn't expect anything else of one's furniture.

But a change has come over the times. Today a wife is known to be a man's partner and timid partners are liabilities.

Self-Confidence and Parenthood

Not only from this material standpoint is the self-confidence of women being taken into consideration, but it is being recognized that from the viewpoint of woman's highest mission—motherhood—it is vital.

It is a well-known psychological law that the mental attitudes of children are largely the result of parental training. A self-conscious, timid mother trains self-consciousness and timidity into her children, and no father in the world wants his children to be that.

So, from money to motherhood, it pays to be self-confident. Not conceited, not vain, not arrogant, but filled with the consciousness of strength.

Self-Confidence Not Conceit

We are always being asked how to differentiate between conceit and self-confidence. This is the difference:

The conceited man tries to make himself *seem larger* by making others seem *smaller,* but the self-confident man expresses faith in his own ability to meet any situation while giving everyone else his chance.

It is his belief in his ***power to win in the open*** rather than any attempt to take advantage, which characterizes the self-confident man.

It is in this sense that we refer to self confidence in this lesson.

The "I-am-the-captain-of-my-soul" attitude, the "unbowed," "unafraid," "master-of-my-fate" conviction is what we mean by self-confidence.

Because it is what you mean also, and what every human being craves, the world has, for this one poem, placed the name of William Henley among the immortals.

Causes of Timidity

Before we tell you how to become self-confident perhaps you would like to know what causes self-consciousness.

It is suggestion. Regardless of what form self-consciousness takes or on what subject the victim is most sensitive, ***suggestion is always the cause.***

William James once said: "No creature is born timid. Look at the naturalness of all animals. Human beings are made timid by suggestions from external sources—people or things. These suggestions literally make the individual 'conscious of self' and there his troubles begin."

The Inlooking Mind

Spontaneity, one of the most attractive qualities, is impossible to the man who is conscious of himself. His mind is always turned inward upon himself instead of outward upon the thing he is trying to do. Consequently, he never does anything effectively.

The Three Elements

Suggestions which make people self-conscious come through various channels. The extent to which any suggestion affects us is determined by three elements—our **respect** for the person or thing **making the suggestion**, the **clearness** with which the suggestion is made, and the degree of our own **sensitiveness.**

The latter element is most important. The very "tough-skinned" are almost impervious to suggestion, while the extremely sensitive individual registers the merest suggestion.

These naturally sensitive men and women are the most wretched of beings. To them the world is a hostile place bristling with inimical, or at best, unpleasant forces. They are constantly being wounded, embarrassed, humiliated.

Timidity a Disease

Many of our students have told us they considered no affliction in the world as bad as their self-consciousness.

They came nearer the truth than they knew. Self-consciousness is a malady amounting almost to a mental disease. It is a fixed, predominant mental attitude which, after a few years, becomes embedded in the subconscious.

Two Young Men

Let us look at two of our young men friends—both well born, well educated, well physically.

One walks down the street with his chest up, his shoulders back, his head high.

He walks as if he were going somewhere, as if he knew where it was and what he was going to do when he got there.

He sees you coming and has a real smile at the bursting point by the time you get there.

He speaks to you dynamically, cordially, and if he is an old friend and has the time he will shake hands.

He probably won't slap you on the back. Jarring your friends' lungs out of place is not as popular as it used to be.

When he shakes your hand you will notice something. He won't crush the bones—that isn't good form any more, either—but you will know something has hold of you. He does it as **though he liked you.** His eye has a sparkle in it, his voice has a ring to it that seems **alive.**

Alive, that's it. The self-confident man or woman simply seems more alive. That's why you like to trust them to **do things.** You believe they can meet emergencies, you have faith in their powers. And whether it is a heart or a job you have to offer, you select this kind of chap to receive it.

What about the other young man? Remember, he has just as much of every material thing as the former—money, clothes, education, looks.

But he walks with his chest down, his head slants a little and a timid look is in his eye. The former

Has he done anything to be ashamed of? No. He is a fine, clean, honest young chap with nothing at all against him.

But he walks and stands and shakes hands as though he owed the world an apology.

Now about this time something has begun to happen in your mind.

Your mental processes have operated at such lightning-like speed you are not conscious of each step, but this is it:

You saw super sensitiveness written all over that young man; you would like to like him, you would like to give him that job, but he seems to be afraid of himself. You can't see why he should be, but, your mind argues, "He knows himself better than I do, so he ought to be the best judge."

Also, you know that whether he is weak or not, as long as he *acts* weak he will never get a hearing ♋♋

You know he wouldn't do for a job requiring initiative for initiative takes a little daring.

You would dislike to have your daughter marry him because you can see him *getting the worst of it from* everybody. If you are the daughter yourself you wouldn't want him for a husband unless you feel you have enough self-confidence for two.

At Your Own Valuation

The fact of it is that the WORLD DOES TAKE US AT OUR OWN VALUATION. It is too busy with its own affairs to take the trouble to investigate us. It prefers to accept us at face value, at least until events prove the contrary.

So the young man with the self-confident manner gets the chances.

Enough chances are all that any of us need. The man who gets them wins. The one who doesn't get them, *no matter how great his natural abilities*, falls behind ♋♋

You Your Own "Ad."

What was it that made you distrust the second young man? It was his *poor advertisement of himself.*

You are your own advertisement. Everything about you is advertising you *all the time*—your facial expression, your walk, your posture, the way your hands act, the way your head sits on your shoulders, the direction your chin points, the tones of your voice, the grip of your hands, the way your feet hit the ground.

Every person is telling what he thinks of himself every waking moment. It is impossible for him to disguise it. He may camouflage one or two elements—such as the tones of his voice or the shake of his hand—but he cannot camouflage them all for there are too many.

Mind and Muscles

Every external muscle expresses *states of mind.* Every thought, however transient, has its corresponding muscular mechanism which reacts instantly and *automatically* whenever that thought flits through consciousness.

In each individual there are millions of these outlets. Each one is a little head gate in the intricate system, and the instant it is unguarded, out flows the betraying expression. A clever man may become adept at guarding the main gates, but they are always being off-set by the opposite testimony from the little ones.

Afraid of Himself

In short, you are advertising your own *estimate of yourself* every waking moment, in ways so glaring that every friend knows what you really think of yourself. Even strangers who pass you on the street know whether or not you believe in yourself 🡂🡂

The timid person is full of fear. He may have unlimited moral courage and often has, but he is *afraid of himself.* This settles into a fixed attitude—the attitude that he is *unequal to the occasion;* that he is going to acquit himself poorly; that he is beaten *before he starts.* With this thought uppermost it is impossible to win. As long as it forms the background of his thoughts it will influence every act of his life. One poet put it this way:

> *"If you think you're outclassed you are.*
> *You've got to think high to rise.*
> *You've got to believe in yourself*

Before you can ever win a prize."

—Walter D. Wintle

The Self-Defeated

No power on earth can save you from defeat if you expect it. Because the man who thinks defeat ACTS defeat.

The man who acts defeated is defeated before he starts ❧❧

But he is not defeated by external things as he imagines. He is defeated by himself.

The self-conscious person is defeated by his self-consciousness. Everyone is aware of it. Some pity him, some despise him, but none dares trust him with responsibility.

Responsibility and self-fear can't work together. So, all the good places go to those who have the self-faith attitude.

Others Affect Our Lives

Ex-President Eliot of Harvard said: "There is no measuring the extent to which other people's opinions of us affect our lives. The impressions others have of us determine, to a great extent, the opportunities offered to us, and these, in turn, determine the heights we achieve."

Did you ever stop to think how everything you want out of life is within the hands *of other people* to give you or withhold from you?

To be sure, no one person or small group of persons can turn the tide of your life permanently, but if we could bring together *all the people* with whom a man has come in contact from the cradle to the grave we would find that his life had been a failure or a success *in proportion* as they had *opened* or *closed* the avenues of opportunity to him.

Your Self-Impression

If we could go a step further and interview every person who had used his influence for or against that man, each would tell us he acted according to the *impression* he had of the man.

Now the impression you make on others is due almost solely to the *impression you have of yourself.* If you are afraid of yourself others are afraid of you; if you trust yourself others trust you. Confidence begets confidence.

Law of Suggestion

Having seen the contrast between the self-confident and the self-conscious, let us look into the law of suggestion, whose workings bring it about. That law is this:

You tend to follow every suggestion made to you unless inhibited by a stronger suggestion in another direction ❦❦

It is not necessary here to go into the ramifications of suggestion-that most powerful combination of forces in our lives-except to point out that every act is, directly or indirectly, *the result of a suggestion* from something or somebody.

Everything from love-making to advertising is based on the law of suggestion.

The most important factor, as before stated, is the sensitiveness or suggestibility of the individual.

Close to this is the element of respect for the person or thing making the suggestion.

Poisoned by Parents

Right here comes one of the most deplorable facts concerning the big question of self-confidence: Most self-conscious people are *made so by their parents* or others with whom they grow up.

The child is taught that he is "too little" or "too young" to do this or that. He is taught *fear* of the dark, *fear* of policemen, *fear* of his playmates, *fear* of his parents, and *fear* of hundreds of other things.

If you wish your child to be thoroughly self-confident see to it that you suggest to him *only those things you wish to see come true in his life.*

Fear and Discipline

With no realization of wrong they are doing, parents who feel unequal to the task of disciplining their children call to their aid the worst enemy of every creature—*the instinct of fear.*

The extent to which this meets with success depends, as before stated, on the sensitiveness of the individual child and the *finesse* with which suggestions are made. The *source* from which the suggestions come is not questioned, because the child trusts his parents implicitly.

As we grow older, we are saved from many dangerous suggestions by our distrust of the person making the suggestion. Even the child learns at an early age the groundlessness of some of these parental bugaboos and thereafter takes everything his parents tell him with a "grain of salt."

How Self-Consciousness Grows

But the self-confidence of the sensitive child is often hopelessly ruined by this time. He has been told so many times "he must not attempt what the others do;" "he might fail and then what would people say;" "he hasn't the ability" to do this or that; "children are to be seen, not heard;" "those people are looking at you," etc.; till he feels all eyes are constantly glued on him, that he is the *center of curiosity and criticism.*

The damage is soon done. These suggestions like all early suggestions, *sink deep into the subconscious* and there form the main-spring of conduct for all later life.

Parents are committing crimes when they SUGGEST WEAKNESS, INCAPACITY AND SELF-DISTRUST TO THEIR CHILDREN ᰣᰣ

Disappointed Parents

All these mistakes are made with the best motives in the world, but *natural law is natural law* and operates without regard to "good intentions." ᰣᰣ

Parents who thus bring up their children under the pall of self-fear, wonder why they do not blossom out self-confident and self-reliant at twenty or so.

The Case of William

Last year the parents of a seventeen-year-old boy brought their son to us for a personal analysis.

"We want you," they said, "to give William your psychological and other tests and tell us why it is that he does not get on better in high school.

"He is all right as far as we can see—perfectly healthy, lots better looking than the rest of those young fellows, if we do say it; has had the very best of home training, and has no bad habits whatever ᰣᰣ

"But he lets the rest of them go clear ahead of him; he always takes a back seat; he won't put himself forward as a strapping boy like that ought to; just won't take part in anything.

"Why, they had some oratorical contests last month and the boy that got first prize does not compare with William. But do you think William would enter? Not for anything! We begged him to, and promised a gold watch if he would, but it did not do any good.

"Now we want to know what ails him." Self-consciousness was all that ailed William. He passed every test ahead of his years. He was far above the average in physique, health, general points and personality.

But when it came to the question, "When you were a small child were you **encouraged** by your parents or **pushed into the background?"** He answered, "Pushed into the background. Dissuaded by father and mother from almost everything I wanted to do."

Further examination revealed that his parents had never permitted him to engage in competitive sports as a little boy.

"Unequal to Emergencies"

Out of several thousands of private students more than half have come to us to be cured of self-consciousness, and of these over seventy percent have answered that they were pushed into the background" as children.

The picture each one of them carried of himself in his mind was that of a person **unequal to emergencies**, and certain to go down before opposition. Staying in the rear and giving front places to others had become a habit.

False Suggestions

Though each case differs somewhat according to the personal experiences of the individual, every person can greatly increase his self-confidence by following the rules laid down in this lesson.

The first step is to realize that your self-consciousness is an **unnatural condition**; that you were not born self-conscious but have been made so by a series of ***false suggestions.*** In other words, the law of suggestion has been used against you.

Your problem henceforth is to reverse that law and make it work FOR you.

The Three Steps

Here are the three stages by which the law of suggestion operates:

Suggestion
Visualization
Action.

The suggestion that you are unequal to the situation brings a mental picture of yourself to fit it—a visualization of yourself as ***weaker than the others*** in that situation.

Every thought tends to express itself in action. Immediately this thought or mental picture of weakness brings forth your actions ***in accordance*** with it. These actions of yours ***betray the state of your mind to others*** and they, taking you at your own valuation, expect you thereafter to ***act self-consciously***

They show that they expect you to act this way. This suggestion from them starts the vicious circle ***all over again.***

You do not consciously figure all this out. You are merely aware that you have acted in a way that did not do you justice. You know you did not express yourself well, did not make a good impression. You are sure others are measuring you accordingly and expect you to play the same role next time.

They show this expectation in various subtle ways. The task of overthrowing their preconceived impressions now seems so great that you do not feel equal to it and fall into the retiring, self-depreciatory attitude permanently.

Your Two Advantages

To pull yourself out of it, reverse the law. It is easier than you think.

You have two big advantages. First, you have your real nature on your side when you start after self-confidence, for self-confidence is *natural to all living creatures.*

Second, you have this advantage: That there is *one* person to whose suggestions you are more *susceptible* than any other. That person is *yourself.* Every suggestion you give yourself affects you more surely and swiftly than those from any other source.

Therefore, to reverse the law, suggest to yourself that you *are* self-confident. This is true. You ARE by nature. You were created that way. But you have been deceived into acting otherwise.

Look back on your experiences and see how unreal, unnatural and *false to your true self* you always felt when you were acting self-consciously.

Recall how self-confidently you perform all acts when *absolutely alone.* This is the ultimate proof that man was born self-confident. Only when he feels the presence of others does anyone feel awkward or embarrassed.

An Instant at a Time

You learned in the previous lesson on "Worry" that you could change the state of your mind at any moment by *changing your attention.*

Transfer your attention for a moment from the idea of self-consciousness to the idea of self-confidence. *Hold the idea for one instant* by your watch and note what happens to you.

We want you to do this *one second* the first time, *two seconds* the second time, *three seconds* the third and so on many times today until you get on "speaking terms" once more with your real self.

Decide What You Want

Tomorrow decide what you **most want to accomplish**, what you wish to become.

Then, in the silence of your own mind, say to yourself, "I shall accomplish that. I shall make this come true."

When a doubt comes creeping into your mind don't let it disturb you. Use the law of attention which you learned in the previous lesson, to turn it away, and go on with your affirmations.

We want you to be a victor in life, and you shall be if you will follow the instructions we give you.

Believe in Yourself

But you must get away from the rag picker's vision you have been holding of yourself. You are not a worm, a crawling thing. You are a human being, created to stand erect and look the world in the face. Start today to lift your chest **and do it!**

If you want people to believe in you, you must **believe in yourself.** You must express that belief by your voice, your walk, your handshake, your bodily posture, by keeping your chin out and your head high.

You must put vim, energy, "go" into all your actions, for these will convince others of your ability who will give you opportunities.

Keeping up the same actions will enable you to make good on those opportunities.

The Winner

The victor, the winner in life's battles, wears **an air of confidence** and assurance. His bearing is one of force, his very presence imparts a sense of power. You spot him as the leader, you would pin your faith to him in a contest.

The vanquished wears the air of defeat, he lacks aggressiveness. Which face do you want to wear?

We ask you to put this face on whether you feel equal to it or not, somewhat as the masquerader dons his for the ball, but with this big difference: You put yours on with the determination *not to take it off,* to keep it there till its shining visage shall become your own.

Think What You Desire

Every time you think of yourself think of *your highest ideal of yourself*—strong, resourceful, influential, successful in just the work you want to do.

If this sounds superficial to you, remember what Professor Munsterberg said to the Harvard students in his class in Psychology: "Young men, whatever you wish to become *begin today* this very hour, *to live that ideal. Act it, think it, talk it,* visualize yourself as that and *that only.* Never let a picture of yourself as *anything else* stay in your mind ๑๑

"If you wish to become a great lawyer start this moment to think of yourself as *already* a great lawyer. Make every action one *befitting a* great lawyer. Make every tone of your voice, every gesture, every posture, every statement you utter, *worthy* of a great lawyer.

"Refuse to admit that you are only a student perhaps earning your way through this institution. See this institution rather as the *alma mater* which gave this great lawyer to the world. In this way have men achieved the impossible."

Rehearse Your Part

If you fail to see the necessity of this, remind yourself that the player whose acting thrills and holds you has achieved it only after *long rehearsals in private.*

Your life is like that. You have played the self-conscious roll because you saw a mental picture of yourself as a self-conscious individual. You can reverse it and hereafter play a self-confident, victorious one by *reversing the picture* of yourself inside your own mind.

Don't Belittle Yourself

Under *no circumstances* allow yourself to think of yourself as a weakling or a failure.

Never make derogatory remarks of yourself any more than you would of others.

Don't criticize yourself to others; don't tell your faults; don't depreciate yourself.

Every time you do these things you are tending to fix upon yourself the weakness of which you accuse yourself; *you tend to become what you say of yourself.*

When people pay you compliments or praise, don't apologize, or blush. Accept them.

If you think they are more than you deserve, *determine to catch up.* Determine to become worthy. But don't deny them.

Self-Cultivation

Take it for granted that you have the self-confidence and enthusiasm *to do what you want to do.* These qualities are there, inherent in you, but they will never come to the surface *unless you expect them to.*

Train your mind deliberately, day by day, *to demand that these qualities come to the top.* Expect them to rise to the surface. Put yourself into situations where you must have them. Then you will see them emerge and come to your rescue!

Why We Fail

The trouble with most of us is that we *save ourselves* from emergencies, we *avoid* crucial situations, we *sidestep* responsibilities and thus *keep submerged the greatest powers we have.*

Nobody ever learned to swim on dry land. You have to plunge in, in order to find your powers.

Nature comes to the aid of him who needs her, trusts her and throws himself on her mercy. She has no use for cowards. She gives all her prizes to those who pitch in and try—to those who dare ♫♫

History's Records

History is full of the proof of these things. Everyone knows that the Spanish Armada, which Philip II fitted out to conquer England, was a miserable failure, not because it lacked material strength but because its commander had *no confidence in his ability to win.*

This commander was the Duke of Medina Sidonia. He wrote the king, in answer to his appointment, saying he was sure to be beaten; that he knew nothing of naval matters; that he was unacquainted with the officers who were to serve under him.

He concluded by saying that he was always seasick on the ocean and that if the king insisted upon sending him at the head of this expedition *it would surely fail.*

Philip did insist, in the false belief that the physical strength of his fleet could offset the fear in its leader. Realization of the power of a man's psychology would prevent such an appointment today. Can you imagine President Wilson sending Pershing to France at the head of the A. E. F. if he had had this attitude?

But Philip manned 130 ships with more than 30,000 men, and over 2,500 guns.

The expedition was the marvel of the times. The English fleet didn't compare with it in equipment, ships or men, but the English fleet won because it was commanded by Lord Howard, who *believed in himself.*

Self-Faith a Magnet

Faith in yourself is the *supremist factor* in your life. It will attract people to you; it will influence others favorably; it will *draw* and command the affection, confidence and admiration of the world. It is a force before which the world bows and in return for which it bestows its *choicest gifts* ❦❦

Not only does this faith in yourself impress others and powerfully influence them in your behalf, but it strengthens and develops *you.* It brings out the best in you.

Fear of yourself crushes, deadens, depresses.

Self-confidence is a *stimulant.* Self-fear is a *deadly narcotic.* You are injecting one or the other of these into your consciousness *every waking moment* ❦❦

"Circumstances"

Get every doubt of your ability out of your system. You are not a victim of circumstances except as you *think so*. When you think you are, your own fear thought is *making* the circumstances.

People who go to the top do not stand around waiting to see what is going to happen. They make it happen. They have *a conviction of their own ability* ❦❦

Study the life of any famous man or woman and you will find every one of them *believed in himself.* Every one of them had confidence in his *power to do.*

Once a colonel came to Napoleon just before a battle. "Are we going to win?" asked Napoleon. We will if circumstances permit," answered the colonel &c&c

"Circumstances!" exclaimed Napoleon, *"I make circumstances!"*

The world might well be divided into two classes—those who let their lives be made by circumstances and those who *make their own circumstances.*

What Do You Want?

The first step in the mastery of your own life is taken when you have fully decided *what you wish to accomplish.*

Then PICTURE yourself as you will talk, act, dress, walk and conduct yourself generally when you have accomplished it.

This is *visualization*, the second great step in the law of self-confidence. Visualization deals with action, it makes you the leading character in your own drama. It sets the stage and gives the other characters their respective roles.

Picture yourself doing *what you want to do*, and because your life follows your thoughts, some day you will be doing it.

Be Definite

If you find it difficult to form these pictures of yourself, it is probably due to your not having *a sufficiently definite idea* of what you want to do.

Go back then to the first stage and make your decision. From that time on *expect yourself to accomplish this.*

In every human being there are enormous untapped resources, undiscovered possibilities, *far greater capacities* than he has dreamed he possessed. Place yourself where they must save you, *where you must sink or swim*, and what happens will astound you.

Your Great Within

"Deep in the inmost recesses of your soul are untouched mines of energy. If you blast deep enough you will find them. But the only thing that ever goes deep enough to bring out the greatest ones is jeopardy.

"The most priceless thing that can ever come into a life is that book, that event, that sermon, that experience, that emergency, that catastrophe—that something which *sounds the depths of a man's nature* and flings wide the doors *of his own great within*," says Orison Swett Marden.

The You of To-morrow

It is not the man you are which is most important to you, but the man you *are capable of becoming*. Place yourself in the situations that will bring out that *possible you.*

This best part of you may be submerged under all sorts of debris—fear, timidity, doubt, uncertainty and self-consciousness—*but it is there.* You can bring it out and place it at the helm of your life *if you try.*

You were born to conquer, to play a leading part on the world's stage. But you will never play it, you will never do anything superb, *until you believe in yourself.*

The story of David and Goliath is not far-fetched. The pebbles of self-confidence in the sling of aggressiveness have enabled many a little man to vanquish a giant.

Take Your Aim Seriously

Show me any great accomplisher and I will show you a man with great confidence in himself, in his aim, and in his own ability.

If there is a link between God and man, it is this thing of self-faith.

Start today toward the realization of the ***things you desire.*** Look upon them as ***possible of attainment.*** Make your visualization of them concrete, practical, and then ***believe*** you can get them 🙘🙘

Many people fail because they look upon their ambition, their life's dream, as a fanciful fiction. They think of it, but only as something which can never be realized. ***They do not take their ambitions seriously.*** We have heard many gifted men and women gently ridicule themselves for their aspirations.

You have got to believe ***utterly*** and ***seriously*** in your ideal before you can ever make it real.

No matter how unconventional, unusual or impossible your ambition seems, don't lose faith in it. The thing you call impossible ***will be done by someone else tomorrow!***

Disraeli's Confidence

Disraeli, a young English Jew, was sneered at one day by a political opponent. "You will be sorry for that," he said, "when I am Prime Minister of England." That any man of his despised race could achieve the highest political office at the command of the proud British nation would have been laughed at as impossible. But Israeli, by his supreme self-confidence, ***did*** become Prime Minister of England!

Act Your Ideal

If you lack this faith in yourself there is one certain way to acquire it. The way is to follow the three steps—suggestion, visualization, action.

Remind yourself every hour of the day that you are a human being and no human being *was ever born timid.* Visualize yourself IN the place you wish to be, DOING what you wish to do, HAVING what you wish to have. Then ACT in accordance with your ideal.

It is not difficult to act in accordance with your ideal if you faithfully live up to the first two stages. Keeping the thought of your ambition before your eyes automatically compels you to act in harmony with it.

Whenever you find it difficult to live up to your expectations it is because you have not etched the picture *with sufficient clearness* in your own mind.

Don't Doubt Your Divinity

Let us beg of you not to yield to the temptation to pass lightly or doubtingly over these great truths. If you do you are cheating yourself.

There is no irony comparable to that of a man doubting his own divinity.

One of the greatest difficulties in the world is to get people to realize *their own bigness.* They are their own jailers.

Perhaps it will help you to see that these statements are not mere vaporings of an optimist, if we quote to you something America's greatest psychologist, Professor William James of Harvard, once said:

"Each of us," he declared, "has resources of which he does not dream. If we could only turn an X-Ray on ourselves most of us would find in the great within of us which may not have gotten even to the germinating stage. There is probably not a living being who would not be amazed if he could see all of the potentialities within himself. If he could he would probably say, 'These remarkable qualities belong to someone who has achieved, not to an unknown person like me.'" ❧❧

Your Gold Mine

The real problem is to know *how to get at* these gold mines within yourself. You can solve that problem if you will follow the instructions in this lesson.

First of all, *refuse to recall the failures* you have made in the past.

Whenever the memory of yourself in a humiliated, dejected state comes to you say to yourself, "That is gone. I shall never appear that way again." ❧❧

Keep your mind on the pleasant memories if you must reminisce.

But if you really want to accomplish something great, remember this: memories, whether pleasant or unpleasant, are *thieves of the mind.*

The past can never be lived again. The future is what counts. Every thought you give to the past *steals the mental energy* you should be devoting to the future.

The Magic of Sincerity

Let us tell you at this point about your chief handicap when you are attempting to act self-confidently. It is this: you do not act *as you really feel.*

If you would conquer self-consciousness, overcome timidity and acquire perfect self-confidence, *never attempt to say things or do things in which you are not absolutely sincere.* In other words, be yourself.

We do not mean by this that you are to be blunt, discourteous, or selfish—quite the reverse. We mean that if you really want to "put yourself over," be sure it is ***yourself and not someone else*** you are trying to put over.

Don't assume unnatural accents. For instance: If you are a Westerner in the East, don't try to copy their broad A's or slight your R's.

You may feel conspicuous at first, but people want you to be natural, not necessarily like themselves. A secret contempt, more or less subconscious, is aroused by the person who tries to imitate others ❧❧

Imitation is undesirable for many reasons, but chiefly because it is ***always detected.*** Any attempt on your part to copy the mannerisms, poses, or attitudes of others is sure to make you self-conscious, and this self-consciousness makes you much more conspicuous than your own attitudes would ❧❧

The very first element of true self-confidence is ***sincerity*** ❧❧

Be Spontaneous

The second is ***spontaneity.*** No one cares to hear what you say if they imagine you do not believe it yourself, but the whole world will listen when you say ***what you earnestly believe.***

Nothing can be so foolish, so ridiculous, that you cannot get a hearing for provided you believe in it ***with your whole heart.***

The next time you meet anybody, the next time you face any situation, ***act out your real self.*** If you will do this you will never appear self-conscious, for your real self is not self-conscious. It is self-confident.

Mingle with People

Mingle as much as possible with other people. Seek opportunities for meeting new people, and when invitations are extended to you by your friends *accept them.* Force yourself to say you will come. Then that promise will help you to silence your weaker self when, as usual, it comes whispering to you not to go.

The Timid Young Woman

We know a young woman not at all industrious, who never feels the urge to work until a social engagement is demanded of her.

She usually refuses, declaring she has "*so much to do* she doesn't see how she can arrange it."

If by any chance she is lured into accepting she almost invariably cancels the engagement later, describing at length the pressing duty which has intervened.

Now this young woman imagines she is telling the truth, but her friends know the real reason is her timidity. She recoils from contact with others. She shrinks from even her best friends. She withdraws into herself and stays there, with the result that she is becoming more and more self-conscious. Her timidity is ruining her life.

You must not only mingle with people when they invite you, you must invite them occasionally, not for etiquette's sake, but because taking the lead will force you to take responsibility and this will bring out your initiative.

After all, it is up to you to do *your share* in the world ☙☙

Psychology of the Timid

Timid people are constantly feeling neglected, humiliated and desolate. They repel advances, yet are hurt when they are not continued.

The sensitiveness which accentuated their timidity in the first place makes them poignantly aware whenever they are left out. But this is the invariable result of timidity.

If you want to be sought after, loved and admired, remember you must "do your bit."

The world does not owe you anything except what you **earn.** If you contribute nothing to the happiness, progress and inspiration of others, after a while no one will contribute these things **to you.**

To Help Others

Most timid people, as we have said before, are more mental, more sensitive, and more sympathetic, than others ☞☞

These qualities make the retiring man a lover of mankind, a sympathizer with the woes, hardships and tragedies of his fellowmen. He often longs to serve mankind, to be an inspiration to the world ☞☞

But the timid man never inspired anybody. In the presence of timidity we are always depressed.

The timid man cannot lead. He cannot even lift because his timidity decreases his strength.

The world's homage, the world's salvation are in the hands of the strong, the courageous—the people of **sublime self-confidence.**

No Bull in a China Shop

To be self-confident does not mean one should be boisterous, bold or scatter things right and left like a bull in a china shop. He must never intimidate others. It means the frank, democratic, sincere **expression of himself.** It means showing the world that he is a **human being,** not an excuse.

God made you. He made you to stand up straight, to look the whole world in the eye, to be a credit to that force which created you.

Some animals walk on all fours, but for several million years now, man has been walking on his two hind legs. Don't let those millions of years of evolution be lost on you!

Don't cringe. Don't crawl. Don't apologize. Don't take a back seat. Don't make excuses. Don't whine. Don't cower.

If you do any of these things here is another don't: Don't justify yourself with any self-righteous excuses ❧❧

If you are timid it is not for any of the reasons you have been giving yourself. It is because you are SCARED.

Fear and Timidity

Fear is at the bottom of all timidity. If you have been salving your sore of self-consciousness with the idea that humility is righteous, start your emancipation today by ***getting honest with yourself*** ❧❧

Humility is ***pride under a cloak.*** Most of the people who prate against pride are ***secretly proud*** of their humility. They make a virtue of their vice and it is the worst vice in the world for it is the vice of fear.

God must love courage or He would not give His richest rewards for it. Certain it is that the courageous man brings God to your mind, expresses godliness and reassures you of your own divinity ❧❧

Don't Be a Worm

"The survival of the fittest" seems to be God's law. It is no accident that the fearsome, retiring, self-effacing, self-depreciatory fail to win even the love that insures reproduction. It is no accident that everything, from a stalk of wheat to a human being, grows ***with its head up***, not down ❧❧

Whenever you meet any one, let him see by your tone, the poise of your body, the expression of your eye, the enthusiasm of your words and the earnestness of your handshake that you are no worm of the dust.

Be sure at the same time to show him that he too is one of God's creatures.

Play Square

Never take another man's share.

Never cheat ❧❧

Never impose ❧❧

These things are done by the man who does not trust himself in the open, who doubts his ability to win under the rules of the game, and are therefore not the earmarks of the courageous, but the brands of the coward.

Give every man his chance.

Give every man his due.

Give every man a boost.

Give every man tolerance—even the timid man ❧❧

But never let any other man *take away your chances* ❧❧

Let him see that you are fair and square but not "easy." ❧❧

Two Cases

Two pictures, one concerning the insignificant things of life and the other the most vital, come to mind ❧❧

The first one is a moving picture of a street car. A group of people are waiting for it. The first one in line is a timid woman. Everyone knows she was the first one there. She knows it herself better than they do. But because of habit she steps back and *lets everyone else in ahead of her.* The last seat is taken just as she gets inside and she hangs to a strap.

The other is a picture of a home where the parents are *always taking a back seat for their children,* always giving up, always sacrificing, always going without necessities that they may furnish their children with luxuries.

As those children begin to grow up, father and mother begin to dwindle in their estimation because they wouldn't take the time or the money from their children to cultivate friends or to keep up with the times. Father and mother seldom go out.

Now people who do not go out among others frequently fall behind.

Father and mother realize this and hesitate to express opinions to these precocious young men and women of theirs.

In a little while father and mother are unmistakably timid *before their own children.* Their admonitions, advice and suggestions have little weight.

The children go their respective ways. The morale of the home is broken, as well as the lives of the parents.

These are two widely different pictures. One deals with the little things and the other with the biggest things in human life.

The woman who lets everyone else have her place on the street car, and the parents, did the same thing—they gave the chance which right- fully belonged to themselves to those to whom it did not belong, who could not profit by it, and who secretly despised them for doing it.

Hold Your Own

In every event of your life, from the smallest thing to the greatest, hold your own. Don't push in ahead of the other fellow. *Take your place in line*; don't take the other fellow's; but don't let even your children *take yours.*

Developing self-confidence is not a difficult task, but it does require patience and intelligent efforts 🙚🙚

Don't hurry ❧❧

Don't be anxious.

Don't strain ❧❧

Don't attempt to change yourself overnight.

Don't be like the man who tried to jump over the hill. He went a long way back and ran so hard that when he got to the hill he was obliged to lie down and rest.

Take It Easy

Don't lose time or discourage yourself by being over-strenuous in following the rules of this lesson. Begin **at the bottom and walk over** the hill.

Do something **each day** in accordance with the rules of this lesson. Start with the easy things and work up to those that are hardest.

Let your self-respect show in your eyes, in the triumphant attitude toward every situation and every individual.

Stop thinking of yourself as a nobody, a weakling and a failure. Whenever this picture comes into your mind, substitute for it the picture of yourself as you LONG TO BE. Hold it there. Don't let anything or anybody make you change the slide, and some day YOU WILL BE THAT PERSON ❧❧

Fear is a Bully

Fear is like worry—a bully. The moment you show you are not afraid of Failure, that instant Failure becomes **afraid of you.** He is a bluff, a phantom **created by your own imagination.**

No matter how many times you have gone down to defeat; no matter how many times you have been conquered, lashed by humiliation; no matter how these things have affected people's confidence in you; take a new grip on yourself, give yourself a chance and in six months you will have altered their opinion of you.

As a matter of fact, other people are not as conscious of you and your mistakes as you imagine. They are busy with their own troubles. They are not thinking of you at all, they are wondering what you think about *them.*

Don't Be Disheartened

If you have lost your money, that means you have really only lost time. You have gained experience which should make your time from now on worth double. You have not lost your life. *Everything else can be retrieved.*

Already you are learning to think right. When you *think right* you can *fight right,* and the man who can fight right wins. Don't yearn for strength, *earn it* ♦♦♦♦

Pictures Come True

The mind is the instrument with which you accomplish any purpose.

If you will keep the picture of yourself as a conqueror before your mind, the picture of your- self as a timid man cannot get in.

To do this will not be easy the first day, but it will be easier the second and after you have practiced it for a week you will be surprised at the ease with which you conquer in the little things.

We once heard a man, whose life had been a failure, boasting of the fact that he had "never fooled himself by building castles in the air."

As he was a man of real ability, we had sometimes wondered why he had failed, but we did not wonder after that remark.

Every man who ever achieved anything did just what we are asking you to do—***built his castles in the air first*** and then put foundations under them ᕙᕗ

Your belief in yourself tells your story, ***predicts it years in advance***, predicts it so clearly that every psychologist can tell about where you will land with any given mental attitude.

Beecher's Experience

The men and armies that triumphed against great odds have always been found to have had ***confidence in themselves.***

When Henry Ward Beecher went to England he once rose to speak before a large meeting which was so opposed to him that it hooted, hissed and yelled ᕙᕗ

But it did not down Beecher. He looked that great audience straight in the eye, not with pugnacity nor defiance, but utter self-confidence. He literally cowed it into subjection.

Then he proceeded to preach for two hours. He was one man. He faced thousands of other men and their hostility ***and won.***

Clemenceau of France, Gladstone of England, Wilson, Roosevelt and Bryan of our own country strikingly illustrate the power of self-confidence.

Psychology at Verdun

It was not the strength of the French that stopped the Germans at Verdun—it was the ***might of mind.*** For days before, the generals sent the affirmation, "They shall not pass" down the line, asking each man to pass it to the next and to repeat it every moment until the battle should come ᕙᕗ

That conviction, flaming in the minds of the French, gave to them, through the law whose mysteries we are unraveling, ***the power*** that brought victory ᕙᕗ

Use Your Knowledge

It is not necessary to solve the mysteries of this great law in order to use it, any more than it is necessary for you to understand engineering in order to drive your own car.

We are discussing practical psychology. We have not space to explain how affirmation and visualization give you the power to do what you affirm. But try it and you will find that ***they do.***

No one knows why this law works. We only know ***it does.***

We want you to let it work in your life. Put it to the test. Try out what we have taught you in this lesson. ***It will remake your life.***

LESSON III

———

How to Have a Good Memory

*"The difference between you and the
well-informed man you envy is that
he remembers things and you don't."*

—Thorndyke

THE subject of memory is fascinating because so much depends upon it &&

Without memory all the knowledge of the ages would be worthless &&

*Wi*thout your own memories you would not know who you are. You would not know your name. You would not know how to find your way home nor be able to recognize your own children.

You would not know, but for this faculty, how to walk, how to read, how to speak, how to carry food to your mouth, how to dress yourself.

Memory is the thing that ***determines identity*** without memory you would be helpless, ignorant, hopeless &&

The success of each hour depends to a great degree on ***profiting by previous experience.***

Without memory you would make the same Mistakes indefinitely.

Without memory you could never learn anything &&

But for memory you would **appear to be an imbecile**, and come very near being one.

Uses of Memory

The importance of a good memory can scarcely be exaggerated ❧❧

Socially, the man who can tell a good story, relate the details of an experience and give illustrations, is always sought after.

In domestic life the failure to remember birthdays and anniversaries has precipitated more than one divorce.

Every housewife knows to what a surprising extent successful home-making depends on remembering the little things that must be looked after ❧❧

In business, references, dates, statistics, facts, conversations and legal points, must be stored in the memory if a man would succeed. He must keep his appointments. He must know not only his own business but the business of his competitor.

In the professions it is equally important. Physicians, dentists, lawyers, engineers, lecturers and others, succeed largely in proportion to their **ability to remember.**

What Memory Is

What do we mean by a memory?

We mean a mental picture. These mental pictures hanging in the gallery of your mind are all that **connect you with the person you were yesterday.** The things you remember from today are all that can identify you with the person you will be tomorrow ❧❧

Memory may be likened to a ***preserving fluid*** that correlates the various elements of the personality and keeps them ***aware*** of each other.

Without the memories you have of yourself yesterday you might as well have been a piece of furniture, a horse or a street car.

Association Centers

It is this cord called memory which ties together the millions of thoughts and experiences of your past and organizes them into groups called ***"association centers."***

Around each event of your life there is grouped the various incidents related to it; around the most important ones are built memories of everything and everybody that was connected with it.

With such perfection has this intricate system been constructed that the mention of one of the smallest elements will bring to mind the central figure. Step by step the wires of memory's telegraph system trace back (in the order in which the events occurred) and pretty soon your mind is at the source.

How You "Remember"

You see the truth of this a dozen times a day. The sight of so insignificant a thing as a pin may suddenly bring back to you the recollection of where you placed an important parcel weeks ago.

Because it all happens so quickly, you imagine your mind jumped from the pin to the parcel in one leap. But if you could slow down and reverse the wheels of your mental machinery as the movie-camera does when they put together again a house that has been blown up, you would see that your mind took dozens of ***logical steps back over the ground.***

The pin subconsciously reminded you of something, which in its turn reminded you of other things, and these reminded you of others, and so on, back to the parcel. It almost seems in such cases that something breaks through the obstruction, and from there on the path is easy.

"Key Words"

Most speakers declare they select a word as a key to whole paragraphs and pages. By keeping this key word in mind everything else follows in a procession.

Trying to recall by force of will is never the best method.

When you have need for remembering something, relax the body and mind as completely as possible. **Avoid concentrating** on anything.

Not always, but in most instances, it will find the scent and follow it back to the thing you want.

Places and Memories

Going back to the place where you last remember having a thing will often start the train of memories of what you did with it from that point onward ❧❧

It is now known that the best way to help a witness remember accurately is to take him back where the events transpired. People who in the court room remember nothing, often over suddenly remember all the details when they return to the spot.

A Popular Fallacy

The notion that to have at one's tongue's end masses of dates, numbers, statistics and facts in order to prove one's intelligence is not only **erroneous** but dangerous. We all have today many more of these than we have any need for.

The aim of this lesson, therefore, is not to teach you how to become a human encyclopedia, but to give you the rules whereby you may cultivate the *kind* of memory which will be of *practical aid* to you in your life.

If you could learn and remember all the facts of history, science, art—everything that has ever occurred since the beginning of time, it would be of no service to you save as you *applied it to your own problems* ◖◖

No amount of information is valuable to you unless it *enters into your thinking*, unless it can be used in the form of *judgments and conclusions.*

Learn What to Forget

Therefore, the first rule we have for you is this: *Do not try to remember everything.*

Never try to remember anything which you cannot use or which you can see no opportunity for using in the future.

You have a certain amount of mental energy. When this is being centered on remembering unnecessary things, you do not have as good a memory for the things which are important to you. The first step in gaining a good memory is to *gain a good "forgetter."*

Deliberately refuse to open your consciousness to irrelevant, isolated or *unessential things*. When they come into your life in spite of this, deliberately forget them. Don't allow them to stay and *clutter up your mind.*

Mental Junk Piles

The average mind is like a huge attic, filled with the debris of the past, jammed with the broken furniture, cracked dishes, and tattered accessories of the years behind us.

Instead of building a bonfire of them, eliminating them from our lives, we strain to retain them, and when some valueless remnant is missing—if we fail to recall a date or a name from those dead years—we say, "my memory is failing."

Make up your mind that you are not going to allow yourself to remember the things **which can do you no good**; that you are going to reserve over all of your mental capacity for storing away the information, facts and data that are necessary to your individual needs and to your particular line of work.

Center Your Memories

Life is short. To make yours a success you have got to be a specialist. But concentrating your actions on a certain specialty will never make an expert of you, unless you also concentrate your *thoughts* on it.

We do not mean that you should become narrow.

But this will not make you narrow. The ramifications, highways and byways of knowledge, into which any speciality leads, preclude narrowness.

Aim and Memory

But we want you to organize your life. To do that you must make every mental faculty **work toward your one big aim.**

Your memory is the servant which must gather together the ingredients of your knowledge, training and education on your particular speciality. If memory spends a large percentage of her time gathering data on matters you will never use, you will not go far in your line.

The man who wishes to become a successful lawyer does not spend half his time in a medical school. To be sure, he may find it necessary sometime to know something about the science of medicine, but when that time comes he studies only those phases of therapeutics which he needs in that particular case. He does not waste time delving into the whole science.

Whether you have such a profession in view or not, you have a specialty. That specialty is to ***make a success of your life.***

Your Memory "Spokes"

To make a success of your life your mind must lay successful plans. It cannot do this if you make of it merely a card index system, or reduce it to the position of a file clerk.

Make up your mind what you are going to do with the years that are ahead of you. Then make everything in your life, directly or indirectly, ***serve that one aim.***

Think of your life as a wheel and make everything build toward one aim as the spokes run into the hub.

How to Read

One of the first essentials in this direction is the ***right kind of reading***. Never, except for relaxation, devote your precious time and your priceless brain cells to reading anything which serves no useful purpose.

Acquire the best books and magazines on your chosen specialty. Then ***keep your eyes open*** as you pass news stands for special articles in all other magazines ❧❧

Lifting "The Gist"

Having done this, learn the second step—how to get everything important out of an article, a chapter or a book ***in the shortest time.***

If you are thoroughly interested in this specialty of yours you will soon develop a surprising alertness for relevant material. Your eye will be able to gather the kernel from a page ***at a glance.***

For every grain of wheat there is much chaff. Learn to lift that grain of wheat the instant you look at a page.

The Four Generations

While we are on the subject of Interest, we will give you the four stages, or ancestors, of Memory. They are:

Desire

Interest

Attention

Memory.

What we ***truly desire,*** we are interested in. We are interested in everything concerning it. Desire, therefore, is the mother of Interest.

Interest is the mother of Attention, for we give our attention to that in which we are interested. Attention is the secret of Memory.

You remember the things to which you give concentrated attention. Lack of attention is responsible for much of what you call your "poor memory."

Usually it is not that you have forgotten. You cannot forget a thing you never knew. If you fail to give a thing your attention you ***never know it.***

How One Woman Does It

A woman in an unusual profession manages to find all the articles, stories and pamphlets on the subject of that profession.

She does not do this by giving ***all her time*** to searching for them. She is busy 12 hours of every 24 in the actual performance of her profession.

But so intense is her interest in it that she spies titles and headings instantaneously as she dashes past the windows of book stores, library shelves and other places.

She has trained her interest upon that one subject for so long that it ferrets out and ***draws to her attention*** masses of information, statistics, etc.

Not only her eyes, but her ears, have been trained as under-servants to Interest.

She may be sitting in the last row of a great audience, but if the speaker happens to make the slightest mention, in the most indirect way, of anything pertaining to her work, she catches every word—the author's name, the subject of the article and ***everything else*** which the speaker refers to in ***connection with it.***

Overcrowding The Mind

This woman makes a practice of keeping her mind clear for the things necessary to her progress as the head of her profession.

She does not fill her mental house with inharmonious mental neighbors, friends, distant relatives or skeletons.

But she keeps plenty of spare rooms ready for visitors—the ***new thoughts and ideas*** of her profession, which may happen along.

Self-Interest and Memory

Self-interest is the mother of Desire. You always remember best that which is ***to your interest.*** You can teach yourself ***almost anything*** if it is of sufficient importance in your scheme of things. This was amusingly illustrated to us in Chicago a few years ago.

The Chicago Hat Boy

A boy stood at the entrance of a huge dining room and took every man's hat. He gave no checks and employed nothing to aid him in remembering to which man each hat belonged.

The men did not come out in the order in which they went in. They wandered out by ones and twos during the course of the next two hours.

Though there were over 200 hats he did not make one mistake. Every man was given his own.

We asked him how he did it. He said that he did not have more than an average memory when he became a hat boy.

But," he said, "I tried trusting to my memory just to see what I could do. It's lone- some standing around here with nothing to do but take hats.

After a little while I told the other boys what I could do. They made bets with me that I couldn't.

"I had to win the bets and after that I began to have a reputation as the boy with the wonderful memory.'

"To live up to it I had to improve my memory, and when I casually mentioned to a man the date on which he was here last, he was flattered, and I gave me a larger tip. ***The more I remember the more I make.***"

This boy's case is a simple illustration of how self-interest aids memory.

Pleasant Memories

Freud, whose writings have advanced the science of the subconscious during the past few years, says, in his "Psychopathology of Everyday Life," page 45: I observed that of a great number of professional calls I never forget any that I was to make on colleagues."

Our *interest* in friends and contemporaries is always greater than in strangers. These are often closely linked with self-interest.

Dr. Ernest Jones maintains that we all have a tendency to forget ***whatever brings unpleasant associations.*** "In my own life," he declared, "I have on numerous occasions forgotten appointments with patients who were very tedious and uninteresting." ❧❧

When You Fell in Love

If you doubt that interest produces attention and attention produces memory, notice with what vividness you recall the dress, the colors and every detail worn by one of the opposite sex after you have ***become interested*** in that person.

Note also your inability to remember what he or she wore on the occasions before your interest was aroused ❧❧

You always give your attention to that in which you are truly interested. You will remember that to which you have been induced to give concentration ❧❧

Al Jenning's Story

Edgar James Swift in his "Psychology and the Day's Work," relates a story told by Al Jennings about how he forced a district attorney to fix his attention upon a wrong date in order to establish an alibi for one of his crimes.

Jennings and his gang robbed a train on October 1st. The next day, October 2nd, Jennings walked into the office of the district attorney and said: "I've been hearing a lot of fool talk about my robbing trains and going on the dodge. I'm tired of it. I intend to surrender, face the music, and clear myself. I've a few things to settle up first, then I'm coming in. This is October 1st; two weeks from today, October 15th, I'll return. Have your officers ready.'

And as I left his office I repeated: "'Make a note of it—*this is October 1st*, and I 'm coming back on the 15th.'". . . .

"'According to expectations, Pittman was so excited at seeing me and hearing of my intentions that the date impressed itself on his mind only as an inconsequential detail.

"'He never thought to look it up at the time, and when I had use for him it was fixed in his mind—*wrong*

"'Going to the saloon of Ike Renfrow, I got him to send for Bob Motley, the sheriff, my father, and my brother John. Motley was my friend; I knew he would not arrest me without a warrant. To them I talked just as I had to Pittman, getting *the false date*—October 1st—into their minds.

"'No one thought to verify my statement of the date. This made a perfect alibi, for the robbery had occurred *eighty miles away on noon of October 1st.*"

The Subconscious Storehouse

Some scientists maintain that nothing we have ever known, heard, read or experienced ever passes entirely out of the mind. They declare that everything you see or hear is filed away in the storehouse of the subconscious.

Swift relates the three following cases, which go far to substantiate this theory:

The Servant-Girl Story

"A young woman of four or five and twenty, who could neither read nor write, was seized with a nervous fever, during which, according to the statements of all the priests and monks of the neighborhood, she became possessed, and, as it appeared, by a very learned devil.

"She continued incessantly talking Latin, Greek, and Hebrew, with most distinct enunciation. . . . .

"The case had attracted the particular attention of a young physician, and upon his statement many eminent physiologists and psychologists had visited the town and made cross-examinations.

"Sheets full of her ravings were taken down from her own mouth, and were found to consist of sentences, coherent and intelligible each within itself, but with little or no connection with each other. Of the Hebrew, a small portion only could be traced to the Bible; the remainder seemed to be in the Rabbinical dialect.

"All trick or conspiracy was out of the question. Not only had the young woman ever been a harm- less, simple creature, but she was evidently laboring under a nervous fever. ...

"The young physician determined to trace her past life step by step.... He at length succeeded in discovering the place where her parents had lived .... and learned from an uncle that the patient had been charitably taken by an old Protestant pastor at nine years of age and had remained with him some years. . . . . .

"Anxious inquiries were then, of course, made concerning the pastor's habits; and the solution of the phenomenon was soon obtained.

"For it appeared that it had been the old man's custom for years to walk up and down a passage of his house into which the kitchen opened, and to read to himself with a loud voice out of his favorite books. . . .

Among the books were found a collection of Rabbinical writings, together with several books of the Greek and Latin Fathers.

"The physician succeeded in identifying so many passages with those taken down at the young woman's bedside, that no doubt could remain in any rational mind concerning the true origin of the impressions made on her nervous system.

"One of the amazing features of this case, is that the woman, who could neither read nor write, ***could not have*** *understood any of the sentences* which she heard and afterward repeated."

Memory's Vault

Your subconscious mind is the ***treasure vault*** of memory. In it is stored every experience through which you have ever passed.

But you have ***lost the combination.***

In this lesson we are going to teach you that combination. A good memory is yours for the making, but no one can make it for you.

We shall show you how. Then you must do it yourself ❧❧

The "flash of inspiration," as the lawyer calls the brilliant thought that wins him his case, does not come from something outside himself. It rises to the surface from the depths of his ***subconscious ocean*** ❧❧

Regaining "Lost" Memories

Swift goes on to say: There are various ways in which 'lost' memories may disclose themselves."

Not infrequently those accustomed to follow trails through dense woods are unable to recall the paths or direction that they took to reach their destination ❧❧

Yet, several years later, when they again set out upon the same trip, the journey is a continuous succession of familiar objects and vistas. Here half a dozen trails cross; but a stone or tree, or some other familiar object, indicates the route, though so far as the traveler is aware he gave no unusual attention to these landmarks when he first took the trip.

But more striking instances are sometimes observed ❧❧

Childhood Memories

"William B. Carpenter has given an interesting case which shows how experiences of childhood may be impressed and conserved, though the conscious mind reveals nothing of them. Later, when a part of the same childhood's experience is again witnessed, the entire scene in all its details, is reproduced as a vision.

The Minister's Story

"Several years ago,' says Carpenter, 'The Reverend S. Hansard, now rector of Bethnal Green, was doing clerical duty for a time at Hurstmonceaux, in Sussex.

"While there he one day went over with a party of friends to Pevensey Castle, which he did not remember ever to have previously visited.

"His conviction that he must have visited the castle on some former occasion-although he had neither the slightest remembrance of such a visit nor any knowledge of having been in the neighborhood before going to Hurstmonceaux—made him inquire from his mother whether she could throw any light on the matter.

"She at once informed him that, being in that part of the country when he was ***about eighteen months old***, she had gone over with a large party, and had taken him in the pannier of a donkey; that the elders of the party having brought lunch with them had eaten it on the roof of the gateway, where they would have been seen from below, ***while he had been left on the ground with the attendants and donkeys.***"

Memory In the Courts

In all courts much depends on the testimony of witnesses. Many a man has been hanged on the testimony of another whose memory was inaccurate.

Numberless men and women have been disgraced for life by the stories of those who ***thought*** they were telling the truth, but whose memories were not good.

For the best illustration of this in psychological literature, it is necessary to turn again to Swift. He says:

The Jester Murder Case

"A few years ago, the writer's attention was directed to a rather remarkable criminal trial.

"In 1871 Alexander Jester started east from Kansas in a light spring wagon with canvas top, drawn by two small ponies.

"While fording a stream near Emporia, as the horses were drinking, he fell into conversation with Gilbert Gates, a young man who was returning from homesteading land in Kansas.

"Young Gates was travelling in what was then known as a prairie-schooner drawn by a pair of heavy horses.

Jester had three young deer in his wagon, and Gates a buffalo calf.

"They decided to travel together and give exhibitions with their animals to meet expenses. When they reached Paris, Missouri, Gates had disappeared.

Jester's explanation, at the preliminary hearing, was that he became homesick and sold his outfit to him that he might hasten home by rail.

"Jester was seen leaving Paris driving Gates' heavy team with his own lighter team tied behind.

"Later he sold the heavy horses and various other articles known to have belonged to Gates, but which he claimed were purchased.

"It is not the purpose of the writer to decide the merits of the case, but rather to call attention to certain exceedingly interesting psychological features 🙚🙚

"Jester was soon arrested but escaped, and was not brought to trial until 1901.

"**Thirty years** had therefore passed since the events concerning which witnesses were called upon to testify.

"Besides, there was a blinding snow-storm at the time when the crime was supposed to have been committed; and, of course, this would have interfered with accurate observation.

Further, when the witnesses 'saw' the things which they related they were **not aware that a crime had been committed.**

"Two preliminary questions thus suggest themselves:

First, would any one note, as carefully as the subsequent testimony indicated, the peculiarities of a chance traveler on the road, especially in a **blinding snow-storm**, and at a time when no reason existed, so far as was known, for **unusual observation?** 🙚🙚

"Second, would observers, under these circumstances, be likely to remember, after a lapse of thirty years, the **minute details** of what they had seen? 🙚🙚

"The incidents were of the unimportant, un-interesting sort that were frequently experienced at that time.

"Even the prairie-schooner could hardly have been exceptional enough to attract special attention, since, as will be seen later, one of the witnesses was taking his wedding-trip on horseback, with his wife behind him on the same horse. But let us turn to the testimony.

"When the trial was held, two women described the **size and color of all the horses,** the **harness** of the heavy team, **the** *figure* and **appearance** of Jester height, a little over six feet, weight about one hundred and eighty pounds, with a **hook-nose, gray eyes, powerful physique, and large hands** ⚬⚬

"They further testified that, looking into the first wagon as it approached, they saw lying in the bottom the outlines of a **human form** with a **buffalo-robe thrown over it.**

"They gave this testimony confidently, **thirty years after the crime**, notwithstanding they were twelve and fourteen years of age, respectively, when the events transpired, and though they were **riding at a canter** in the face of a heavy snowstorm, with **veils tied over their faces**, and the horses which they met were traveling at a **fast trot** when they passed in the storm.

"A farmer swore that the buffalo-robe was **covered with blood,** and still another witness that, while helping Jester start his wagon, the canvas blew back and he saw the **body of a man** with his throat cut. The description of the body was that of young Gates.

"A man who had just been married, and was taking his wife behind him on his horse to their new home, described the horses attached to each wagon, the wagons, and **the dog**, and this in spite of the fact that his own horse was going at the single foot' gait, that Jester's horses were trotting past, that it was **snowing hard**, and that, being on his honeymoon, **other thoughts and interests** would seem to be occupying his mind ⚬⚬

"A man of thirty-six, who consequently was six years of age at the time of the crime, testified that later during the thaw and heavy rains of spring, he and his father saw the body of a young man of eighteen or twenty years of age floating down the stream.

"He described the **color of his hair and complexion** and said that he had on a **blue-checked shirt** and **blue overalls**.

"His description of the shirt agreed with that of Mrs. Gates of a shirt which she had made for her son

"It is interesting to note, in this connection, that neither the father of the six-year-old boy nor the girls who saw the outlines of a human form in the wagon, nor the man who helped start Jester off, said anything about their observations *until Gates' disappearance nor Jester's arrest had been published*.

"It is quite evident that, whatever the merits of the case, the testimony of these witnesses, after a lapse of thirty years, was amazingly exact. Yet it would be unfair to assume that they were dishonest

All of those from whose testimony we have quoted were people of good standing in the community. They could be relied upon both in word and deeds

The attorney for the defense in the case speaks in the highest terms of these witnesses. 'They were among the best people of Monroe County,' he says. They wanted to be truthful, and they were very friendly to me, entertaining me overnight when I was looking up evidence preparatory to the trial.'

The Explanation

"What then was the explanation of their remarkable exactness, even in the *smallest* and in some instances least *noticeable* and least interesting details?

The key to the mystery lies in the way in which the case was *worked up*, in the *publicity* that it received, and in *human psychology.*

"After Jester's final arrest, Pinkerton detectives were employed and seven or eight leading criminal lawyers of Missouri and Chicago were engaged to assist the prosecution.

"The detectives, as they secured one fact after another, culminated the information by *suggestive questions* and statements to those with whom they conversed ❧❧

"When, for example, a prospective witness said that there was a buffalo-robe in the wagon the detectives would ask if it *covered the outlines of a human form.* The man would think it **likely**, and soon that it *did.*

"Of course, the case was featured in the county newspapers. It was a first-class news story. Pictures were published, pictures of Jester and Gates, pictures of the horses and wagons, pictures of the dog, and pictures of scenes in the chain of events leading to the alleged crime. The pictures were based on what witnesses *said* they saw, and what the detectives said they must have seen, and no reportorial imagination whatever was lacking.

"The clothing of Gates was described, the articles he had with him enumerated, the facts to which certain witnesses would swear were told to other witnesses and reported in the newspapers.

"Indeed, all the events of the crime as it was conceived by witnesses, reporters, and detectives were *portrayed and described* with much the effect of a moving-picture representation, *until fact and fiction were indistinguishable.*

Psychology of Repetition

"It is a well-known principle of psychology that if you tell a man something *often* enough he finally accepts it; and as he continually repeats it, even as a possible fact, it ends by becoming firmly fixed. Then he *believes* that he saw or heard it ❧❧

We must not forget that all this happened thirty years after the events. The undetected *vagueness of memory-details* of the witnesses furnished a fertile soil for the growth of *imaginary pictures*

"The attempt to see faces in the moon is comparable to their experience.

"With a dim outline, or a sketch with several possibilities, there is always a strong tendency to *fill in* the outlines, usually with what is **in one's mind**

"As an illustration, ask a group of persons to indicate the kind of a figure six which is upon their watch-dial. They will be found to divide between VI and 6.

"A few, whose memory is more accurate than that of the others, recalling that the figures take their line of direction from the center of the dial will write the figure upside down.

"All, except those to whose attention the peculiarity has already been called, will 'remember' seeing the figure.

"Yet, in watches with a second-hand *there is no six.*

Perversions of Memory

"Despite the best intentions of truthful people there are many ways in which the memory may be disturbed without the individual being aware of the alteration. A brief reference to some of the causes of these memory distortions will reveal the fickleness of this reproducer of past experiences.

"These alterations of memory have a bearing upon reports of events given either as sworn testimony or in social intercourse, and all are intimately related to the psychology of the day's work

"One of the causes of unintentional perversion of memory is the *constant talk* that an exciting occurrence produces.

"There is always a tendency to say what we *wish might have happened.* This is especially true when we ourselves participated in the events.

"'The most frequent source of false memory,' says James, 'is the accounts we give to others of our experiences. Such accounts we almost always make both *more simple and more interesting* than the truth.

"'We quote what we should have said or done rather than what we *really* said or did. In the first telling we may be fully aware of the distinction. But, ere long, the *fiction expels the reality* from memory and reigns in its stead alone.' It is not necessary, however, that we be participants in the events ❦❦

"The tendency to *enlarge* upon a story is human. So strong is this inclination that if there is nothing unusual in the occurrence the story- teller transforms the common into the uncommon.

"This is especially true when the marvelous is involved. Man is saturated with the mysterious."

Wishes Affect Memory

The explanation of the exaggerated testimony given by these witnesses in the Jester trial is one which applies more or less to everyone.

We are all inclined to let memory trick us into believing we really saw what we wish we had seen.

If we see only a small part of a great catastrophe, such as a fire or an accident, the *desire* of the mind to have seen it all will incline even the most truthful person to believe next day that he saw a *little more* of it than he really did.

If he recounts the occurrence, adding the scenes which he failed to see but which he heard others describe, the day after that he will almost believe he *saw them himself.*

If he has occasion to repeat the narration many times, a week later the average person will be telling the whole story *as though he saw all of it.* This will be especially true if no moral issue is involved and no harm done to any one by the exaggeration ❧❧

A month later you would have a hard time convincing him that he did not see it all. The gaps between the scenes he actually did see would be by that time so *perfectly filled* in by the mental pictures which his *own talking* had painted, that he could not distinguish clearly between them.

The Runaway

A young man of our acquaintance saw a run- away horse dashing down the street with no driver.

Around the corner, a block away and entirely out of sight, the driver, who had been thrown from the wagon, was describing in a sensational way his collision with another vehicle, how the horse became frightened, how he tried to keep control of him and how he was finally thrown out.

The young man who had seen only the horse, came up just in time to hear the man giving these descriptions ❧❧

So vividly did he describe them, and so much did the young man regret not seeing them, that next afternoon he told a group of his friends about the affair, beginning at the beginning and *making himself a witness to the entire accident.*

He was not an untruthful young man, but he was young. We all long to participate in thrilling, sensational, mysterious adventures, especially in youth. Desire, which figures prominently in all memory, was so great in this young man that he believed he actually *had seen* the runaway *from the time it started.*

The Real vs. The Unreal

In recollecting anything, we are inclined to place the interpretations *we prefer* on events. In a little while we find it impossible to distinguish between **what actually occurred** and **our thoughts about** what **might** have occurred.

To be sure, wishes, desires, preferences control our interpretations of every event of life to a **far greater extent** than we realize.

What psychologists call a retroactive memory sometimes steps in and fulfills these hopes in our minds ❧❧

Thinking of what we wish we had done on a certain occasion, we think that action into our series of memories.

Transposing Events

The mind also has a habit of **transposing** our experiences and inserting them in the chronological order in which we wish they had transpired.

For instance, witnesses often testify to having examined the spot where the murder was committed. In their testimony they insert their examination **after the crime**, for that lends a more **dramatic element** to the story.

Psychology of Prejudice

Bias, prejudice, preferences of all kinds blind us to details opposed to those prejudices. Often we do not intentionally shut out these details. They are shut out for us by that little doorkeeper of our subconscious mind, "Attention."

Let two people hear a lecture, one disliking, the other liking the speaker.

On the way home the one who was fond of the speaker will refer to his pleasing manners, attractive dress, charming personality and distinct voice. The other will be unable to remember these points, even though the efforts of the speaker in these directions were so great as to be **apparent to everyone else.**

The same is true of the arguments brought forth ❧❧

Debates and political rallies significantly illustrate how we see what we *wish* to see, hear what we *wish* to hear, and *forget the rest.*

A Republican and a Democrat go together to a Democratic meeting.

Next day the Democrat will recall only those points and incidents which aided the Democratic side &&

The Republican will have forgotten them, but will distinctly remember any misstatements or derogatory incidents.

Hearing these two men describe the evening's events you would never guess they were describing the same rally.

Mountains and Mole Hills

To a man who wishes to believe a thing, every small incident is *significant* evidence, just as, to him who does not wish to believe it, *nothing* is sufficient to make it seem true.

The psychology of college debates years ago convinced us of this. Whether our team won or lost, we remembered only the good points it had made, those places where it *distinguished itself,* those refutations in which it was most brilliant.

If one of our speakers achieved a moment of real victory we recounted it with such fervor that to our listeners it outweighed the adverse decision of the judges. In fact we almost forgot that the decision went against us.

How hard it was to recall the telling points made by the opposing team! For the life of us, and in all sincerity, we *couldn't remember them!*

Forgetting The Unpleasant

Memory keeps green the pictures of our triumphs, unless the individual is inclined to morbidity, and then it keeps alive the incidents in which he failed &&

In either case, however, it is the same law of desire in operation. The morbid individual **prefers** to recall the unpleasant. He gets a kind of pleasure from his own suffering.

The forgetting of anything to which one has given attention at the time of its occurrence is often due to a subconscious desire to forget it.

This interesting phenomenon is seen many times a week in the lives of each of us.

You are likely to forget a man's name if, upon being introduced to him, you form a **dislike** for him. If, in the back of your mind, you prefer not to know him you probably will **not** know him the next time you meet him.

If you are given unpleasant tasks to perform, such as mailing your wife's letters, no impression she can make on your mind will be as vivid as those connected with pleasant tasks.

Everything which evokes painful feelings is more easily forgotten than those which bring pleasant ones. An engagement you prefer not to keep is the one you **actually forget.**

Three Laws of Memory

We will now give you the three fundamental laws of memory in their order:

Attention

Association

Repetition

When you have decided that you wish to remember a thing, that it is conducive to your interests to keep it in mind, give it your **undivided attention.**

Turn the lens of your mental camera, of which we told you in a previous lesson, directly on the thing you wish to remember. Close the shutter until your mind is focused **directly and exclusively** on that one thing.

Keep it there for the space of an instant, then tie it up mentally with something else—associate it with something, relate it to something *already in your life.*

For instance, if you are reading an important fact in a trade magazine, get the fact clearly in mind.

Then do not leave it isolated, but decide then and there *in what connection* you will probably make use of that idea.

The Lecturer's Story

It may be of help to you for us to use here the personal illustration of another lecturer in whose repertoire there are over sixty lectures. Not a sentence in one of these sixty lectures is memorized, yet she is never at a loss. She says:

"I was not born with more than average memory powers. In fact I was often impressed as a child with the deficiency of my memory.

"After several years of newspaper work in which I relied on notes exclusively, (giving my memory little to do) I found myself unable to remember names, faces, dates or events.

"At about this time I entered public work, the two chief requirements of which were that I *remember names and faces and make interesting, accurate, extemporaneous* speeches. I will tell you how I mastered the lectures.

"Knowing that my future success in life depended largely on the success I made of this work, the first element—that of *self-interest*—was present ❧ ❧

"The second element—*desire*—was there because I very much wanted to do that particular work ❧ ❧

This, as always, gave rise to the third state—*interest in my subject.* No matter where I was, what I was doing, with whom I was talking, that interest was never out of my mind.

"To get new angles on my subjects I induced people to talk about them, and I read everything I could find on such subjects.

"When a remark or a sentence struck me as being valuable, I gave it such **white heat concentration** that I literally burned it into my mind.

"But I did not stop at that. I decided then and there in which lecture I would use that idea. Not only that, I decided **under which heading** in the lecture that particular idea belonged. I visualized myself **saying it**, I pictured the effect on my audience. I heard in my mind the sentence with which I would introduce it, and something of the words with which I should clothe the idea itself.

"With that I left it, **trusting my memory absolutely** to remind me of it at that particular point in that lecture.

"On the day of the lecture I went over in my mind the respective sections. These ideas invariably came to my mind and came out in my speech that evening as smoothly as those I had expressed before."

Related Pictures

Remember that all memory is a series of related pictures, and to be sure of remembering anything you must connect it arbitrarily or otherwise with **something you already have.**

The content of your mind is like a community in which every person is related directly or indirectly to some other.

Whenever you wish to remember a new idea, marry it to some of these friends.

If there is something you wish to remember to do connect it with something by deciding the **time** or **place** to do it. For instance, tell your mind to remind you, when you reach a certain spot opposite the post office, to turn in and mail the letters.

When you get opposite the post office the sight of that particular spot will usually remind you of the errand.

Analogy and Memory

The importance of association is proven in this: That your knowledge about anything, no matter what it is, is merely a knowledge that it is like something else or **different from** something else.

One of the most important laws of memory is that of habit.

In obedience to this law, the first idea to enter your mind after you see a certain thing will be the one you have **most frequently associated with that thing** in the past.

The sight of a flower will bring to your mind the fragrance of that flower. The fragrance will bring the thought of perfumes, and this will bring to mind the perfume you are in the habit of using.

The word "coffee" will suggest to each individual the particular cup of coffee he is in the habit of having.

The mention of buying a home would bring to your mind the particular neighborhood which you have been in the habit of visualizing as the site of your future home.

"Shoes" will bring to the mind the particular make you have been buying lately.

"Tires" will remind you of the brand you are in the habit of using.

Habit and Memory

It is well known that typists or pianists who have learned one system of fingering find it difficult to change because each letter or note is associated with a certain movement of a certain finger. Habit has so welded them together that when one enters the mind the other responds automatically.

The law of association expresses itself to you a hundred times a day. "Henry Ford" brings to your mind the picture of a little automobile.

When we say "Cream of Wheat" you see the smiling face of a negro waiter. When we say "Y. M. C. A." you see a red triangle, and when we say "Y. W. C. A." you see a blue one.

Because all of these have been associated in your mind you cannot think of one without thinking of the other.

An "Association" Test

Here is an exercise which will show you what we mean: Memory and brains—brains and head—head and headache—headache and doctor—doctor and medicine—medicine and bottle—bottle and wine.

You can remember instantly that we used the word "medicine." You also recall whether or not we used the word "woman."

Repetition under the right conditions is the third step in perfecting the memory. We say "right conditions" because it is now an accepted fact that mere repetition, ***unless coupled with interest***, does not make one remember.

About Memorizing

Do not attempt to cultivate your memory by "memorizing a few lines each day."

It has been shown that no amount of such mechanical gymnastics improves the memory.

Save your mental strength for the many things for which you will have some ***actual use*** in your daily life, and to which you find it easy to give attention ❧❧

Adult Memories

That children have better memories than adults is an exploded theory. Many investigations have been made by the most careful scientists with the result that it is now maintained that the capacity to remember everything of importance in an individual's life *improves throughout his life* up to the time when his mental powers in general begin to decline.

Children excel in rote-learning only, and this because they are accustomed to that particular kind of memory work.

Adults remember with greater facility than children for several reasons. First, they have greater *ability for concentrating their attention, second, their self-interest is keener,* and third, their knowledge with its wealth of *associations* is wider ❧❧

The capacity for reflection, concentration and ambition varies with the individual, but adults have on the whole greater memory powers.

Eye or Ear-Minded?

In cultivating memory, it is of the greatest importance to know to *what kinds* of sensations you respond easiest and quickest. It goes without saying that the particular thing which habitually gets your attention quickest comes to you via the avenue of your *most responsive senses.*

Many people remember best what they *see*; others remember more clearly what they *hear*, though the latter are decidedly in the minority. The first are called the "eye-minded," the second, the "ear-minded."

We have a friend who can never remember what she must get on a shopping tour, no matter how many times she tells her friends or herself what it is she wishes to purchase. But, if she once makes a list of them, she can remember every item if she happens to leave the list at home.

The explanation of this is that she is "eye-minded." No amount of telling or being told can make a clear impression on her mind, but the mental picture of the list is so vivid that the items recur to her in the exact order in which they were written.

We have another friend who remembers best what he hears. All people who learn to play musical instruments "by ear" are decidedly "ear-minded."

Reciting from Memory

In reciting a poem which one has memorized he usually has each stanza photographed in his mind and reads it aloud to his audience line for line from the page in his memory.

This fact explains the ineffectiveness of memorized speeches. The audience is aware of being **read to** out of the speaker's memory instead of being **talked to** out of his heart.

Tests for Eye-Mindedness

If you do not know whether you are eye-minded or ear-minded, here are some tests:

Can you remember how the breakfast table looked this morning?

Can you imagine a street car in motion?

Can you picture the distance between the post office and your home?

If you answer "No" to these questions you are deficient in eye-mindedness.

Can you picture a hurricane in motion?

Can you remember distinctly the different scenes around your childhood home?

After reading an article in the newspapers, have you a keen memory as to where it was located on the page?

If you answer "Yes" to these questions you are above the average in eye-mindedness.

Tests for Ear-Mindedness

Can you, in imagination, hear the telephone bell ringing?

Can you remember the voice of a relative you have not met for six months?

If you answer "No" to these questions you are deficient in ear-mindedness.

Can you mentally hear the breathing of a sleeping child?

Can you in your mind hear thunder?

Can you recall the notes of a selection of music played on the violin?

If you answer "Yes" to these questions you are above the average in ear-mindedness.

To know whether you are more "ear-minded" eye-minded," recall which you remember best, *printed* words or *spoken* words.

Memory Your Secretary

Your memory, as explained before, is one of your mental servants. Treat it as you would any other servant if you expect really good services

Your memory is your private secretary, file clerk, office boy, your mental library, all in one.

Suggestion and Memory

If, upon securing important papers, a busy man sent for his secretary, handed them to her and said, "Here are these papers. I shall want them some time; I do not know when, but someday I shall need them. Here they are.

"You are inefficient; you always fail me; you never can lay your hands on things when I want them, so I don't suppose you will be able to find when I call for them."

If he mentioned to a friend sitting near, "You know this secretary of mine is worthless; I can't depend on her at all".... do you think she would produce those papers when he needed them? She might, but the chances are she wouldn't.

Memory, like other mental faculties, is responsive to suggestion, and especially to **auto-suggestion**

If, on the other hand, he said to his secretary, "Here are some important papers. I have no idea when I shall need them but the time will come. Put them away and I will ask you for them some time. You are such an efficient secretary I know I can depend upon you to produce them when the time comes."

If he also said this to a nearby friend in the secretary's presence, it would act as a further incentives

Your memory must be treated in exactly the same way

Give it **clear, distinct information.** If you are eye-minded, get a clear mental picture of it.

If you are ear-minded associate it with sounds or whatever auditory images you prefer.

Say to yourself, "I will remember that when I need it. When the time comes my memory will know just where to lay hands on it."

To Remember Names and Faces

Here are the five laws for remembering names and faces:

1. Bear in mind that to remember names and faces is **vital to your success** in any line of work, socially or financially.

In other words, realize that your self-interest will be greatly sub served if you can recall, on sight, the names of people you have met.

This fact is based in a psychological law. ***Everyone likes to be remembered***; it flatters his vanity, it appeals to his ego, and at the same time increases his respect and admiration for you. His ego never quite forgives you if you fail to remember his name.

2. When a man is being introduced to you be sure you not only hear his name clearly but know how it is ***spelled.***

If there is any doubt in your mind, ask the man himself to pronounce his name for you and spell it for you. Never ask this of the man who has done the introducing. That is a reflection on him. The other man will be glad to tell you because you are discussing the one subject in which he is most interested—***himself.***

Of course, if his name is Brown it will not be necessary for you to ask him the spelling, for the minute you hear it the little printers in your brain set it up in type and hold it before your mind's eye. But if his name is a long or complicated one, do not consider that you have been introduced to him ***until you know how he spells it.***

3. With the spelling clear in your mind, give your concentrated attention to his face. Look at him and speak to him ***while you are looking at him.*** Connect the name with that face.

If you are ear-minded, it will help if you make him speak to you. Then you will have a voice to associate with the name.

4. Do not keep reminding yourself of his name. Simply file it away in your memory, knowing you will remember it the next time you see him.

5. Whenever you meet him make it a point to ***address him by name*** at the beginning of your conversation ❧❧

Your ability to memorize will increase with the demands you make upon it.

Rely on your memory. Place yourself in positions where it must save you, and it will do it.

Memory is like every other faculty—it develops with use. It grows with the demands made it. It comes to your rescue and reveals its highest powers only in emergencies.

Two important general laws of memory are:

1. Don't worry about your memory.

2. Never say to anyone, "I have a poor memory." &

LESSON IV

——

How To Be Well

"The man with educated bowels will eclipse the man with educated brains, but why not have both?"

—Elbert Hubbard

EVERY human being has a right to a strong, healthy body. Nature starts ninety-nine percent of us with good working capital, and we proceed to do what people usually do who inherit wealth—squander it extravagantly—and as a result are physical bankrupts early in life.

Kinds of Diseases

There are two kinds of diseases—organic and functional

୬୬

Organic diseases are those like tuberculosis, in which there is actual destruction of tissue. Functional diseases are those like constipation, in which there is no actual loss of tissue, but in which some organ fails to perform its natural function.

The average individual pays large doctor's bills each year for having someone with an M. D. help him get over such ailments as constipation, neuralgia, headaches, insomnia—things that arise merely from *slovenly internal housekeeping.*

By following the sane, simple rules laid down in this lesson, the average man and woman may get and keep good health through a long life.

Health and Happiness

Be first of all a healthy animal. Your success and happiness depend more upon your health than upon anything else in the world. It is the real foundation upon which the structure of your life rests ✻✻

If you are thoroughly well, no hardship, no sorrow, no misfortune is great enough to conquer you. If you are sick, no amount of wealth can make you happy.

Yet the average man neglects this greatest of all treasures. He eats anything that tastes good; he eats large amounts of food at one sitting; he breathes any kind of air that happens to be around and uses, on an average, about one-third of his lung capacity.

Man can live only four and one-half minutes without air; he has been known to live forty days without food. Most people almost forget to breathe but imagine they feel themselves getting weak if they miss "three squares" a day.

Motion and Emotion

Exercise in some form is necessary to the health of every individual. Motion must be made to balance emotion if you are to stay well.

But most people do not know this. The man who leads a sedentary life during the day finds sedentary amusement in the evenings at the theatre, or by other indoor diversions.

The average individual drinks about four glasses of water each 24 hours, forgetting that next to air water is the greatest physical necessity, since almost 70 per cent of the human body is water ✻✻

Instead of getting a sane amount of sleep he goes to bed when there is no other place to go and takes a chance on feeling all right the next day.

What Wrong Work Does

As long as men and women follow lines of work for which they are not fitted they will hate their work. The man who hates his work feels that his real life is lived between office-closing time in the evening and office-opening time next morning. He feels that his only chance for happiness is during these hours and uses them accordingly.

That this unfits him for promotion, cheats him out of his chances, robs him of the opportunity to find his right place are facts which short-sighted man fails to see until it is too late.

Heads and Stomachs

Someday the knowledge of how to be well, get well and stay well will be disseminated by our government as one of the highest duties the people can perform for their own preservation and efficiency ৬৬

Children will be taught the rules for healthful eating, drinking, sleeping, exercising and breathing before their A. B. C's.

What Johnnie gets into his stomach will be recognized as of equal importance with what he is getting into his head, because the proper functioning of Johnnie's head is largely dependent upon the proper functioning of Johnnie's stomach.

Some day we will recognize that what Johnnie drinks vitally affects what Johnnie thinks.

You can't divorce your body from your brain. They rise or fall together. Your mind manifests itself through your body. It is the house in which it dwells ৬৬

Because it so vitally affects your mind, this first lesson in psychology, "the science of the human mind," must be devoted to your physical condition.

Running Your Car Right

We all want to get somewhere. Each of us has a destination in view. Your body is the car that must carry you there. You are in a race—the race of life—in which competition is keen and getting keener every day.

No sane driver would run on the rims or fill the gasoline tank with adulterated stuff. Yet most of the failures in this race of life are doing these very things. Then they wonder why they are outdistanced &

In this lesson we are going to give you the sensible, scientific rules by which you can keep your car in good running order.

Breathing

First of all—breathe! Your lungs are your bellows and you must keep them full of air just as the blacksmith does when he is forging.

It takes white heat to forge anything worthwhile. Your mind is a dull ember when your lungs are half empty.

To breathe right all you have to do is to raise your chest. Don't throw your shoulders back violently or make hard work of it. Simply keep your chest up.

Nature does everything else. Because your breathing is the most important thing, she does not leave it to you. She keeps your lungs going just as she does your heart.

In return for her care the least you can do, and in fact all she asks you to do, is this: lift your chest and keep it lifted, so that the thorax, the little room inside your ribs, is not too cramped for expansion &

The Need for Oxygen

Oxygen is necessary to the life of every organism, from blades of grass to human beings, and oxygen can best be had in fresh air.

See to it that the air you breathe is as fresh as possible. We do not mean that you should be fanatical about this or anything else. Don't be freakish and try to live exclusively out of doors. Man has lived for so many centuries in houses he is no longer able to cope with the elements barehanded

But ***circulating air*** that is not too warm is absolutely essential to physical and mental efficiency

This is practical psychology, so do not go to extremes. Do not freeze in order to have fresh air. Have your rooms comfortable but be sure of proper ventilation. Windows slightly open at opposite ends of your house or room will ensure this

It is a bromide to say "sleep with windows wide open," but it is necessary to repeat it often.

Your health is measured by the proportion of ***new fresh cells*** in your body to the ***diseased and dying cells***

Every time you take a lungful of fresh air it produces twenty million new red corpuscles for your blood and carries away as many dead ones.

Breathing Affects Moods

While we are on the subject of breathing, do not overlook the fact that your breathing and your mental state are closely related. Fear, anger, jealousy, worry and all negative mental attitudes are conducive to the stooping posture and to deficient breathing

An inkling of this relationship was had by the ancients. For centuries it was believed that the breath was an expression of the soul. Some occult religions of today are founded on this.

There is at least this to be said for them: your efficiency as a human machine is largely determined by your intake of air, and whether your breathing is or is not related to the soul, it certainly is the infallible indication of the state of your mind.

Joy, happiness, exultation are expressed by the long, deep breath, while their opposites instantly cause a shortening of breath, choking or sobbing ❧❧

Try This

As a mechanical aid to composure and to rid yourself of any negative mental attitude, try forcing yourself to take deep breaths of fresh air at your open window. You will be surprised at the change it will make in your feelings in five minutes ❧❧

Whenever you are in a tight place, whenever you are facing any critical situation, watch your breath. Keep your lungs full, your chest up, your chin out, your head high, and see what wonders it will do for you.

Breathing and Thinking

Breathing impure air powerfully and harmfully affects the mind. Oxygen feeds the fires which burn up the poisons of the body. When these poisons are not properly burned up (oxidized) they remain in the system to depress both mind and body. If you want rapid and healthful mind action you must have oxygen in your lungs.

There is an old saying that deep breathing brings deep thinking and shallow breathing, shallow thinking ❧❧

Despondency, the "blues" and melancholia are characteristic of people who breathe only with the upper part of their lungs.

Clear thinking is possible only when good blood is circulating at a good rate through the brain. Deep breathing not only purifies the blood but pushes it rapidly through the brain.

"Catching" Colds

The old idea that colds come from draughts is today largely discredited. If your body is in a healthy condition draughts will not give you colds. Outright exposure will, but moving air is health-full, not harmful.

You catch some of your colds from sitting in air that is not in motion, air laden with impurities, but only when your physical health is at a low ebb of resistance.

Right here is perhaps the best place to tell you exactly what causes most of your colds. That cause is constipation, and constipation comes from ***wrong eating***. Nothing short of a blizzard or a drenching rain will give you a cold unless you are constipated. If you are constipated, not even a draught is necessary.

You "catch cold" from the poisons which your clogged-up colon sends through your body.

Therefore, reverse the process when you get a cold and stop eating; take an enema to rid the system of the poison already banked up, and give the system a chance to clear itself of debris before putting any more food into it.

Food Poisons

Most food is thirty-five per cent poison, and as such, has to be disposed of. A cold is unmistakable evidence that your body is already overloaded with poisonous materials. Give it a chance to clear the decks."

Don't let your friends tell you that you "must eat." ❦❦

If you stopped eating at this moment, did not eat a mouthful for a week, and took nothing into your stomach but water, you would have plenty of strength for carrying on any ordinary work.

When this is true of the man who works you can see how exaggerated are our notions about the necessity of eating.

Front and Back Doors

Any person in average health has sufficient strength already stored up in his system to carry him safely through several days of fasting.

The man with a cold, therefore, does not need more strength, but less poison.

Nature is a marvelous restorer. She disposes of unbelievable quantities of poisons when given the chance ❧❧

But if you eat when you have a cold you are shoveling debris into the front door faster than she can carry it out at the rear.

The old saying "stuff a cold and starve a fever" is used in the opposite sense from what was meant originally.

The original saying was: "If you stuff a cold you will have to starve a fever,"— it being well known that a neglected cold sometimes leads to a fever.

Colons and "The Flu"

La Grippe is a cold in an exaggerated form. The devastating Spanish Influenza is the same thing carried to "the third degree" and is nothing more nor less than La Grippe in a malignant form ❧❧

It is now well known that not a trick of fate, but the condition of the colon and intestines, largely determined whether or not one had the "flu." That the "flu" was somewhat contagious cannot be denied, but whether or not one "caught" it depended on the condition of his colon and intestines 🙠🙡

Colds and Cleanliness

The time is coming when instead of sympathizing with the individual who has a cold we shall recognize that he is unclean internally and deserving of the same opprobrium as the man who is unclean externally.

Sleeping out of doors, exercise in the open air and the avoidance of too much protein food are other means for avoiding colds.

Eating—Favorite Indoor Sport

Baseball may be the favorite outdoor, but eating is the favorite indoor sport of Americans.

It is estimated that the average man and woman in this country eats twice the amount of food necessary to health, while many, especially among the well-to-do, eat five times as much. Until people realize the danger in this procedure they will continue to do so because they have the greatest urge toward it.

All instincts are hard to combat because they are so deeply imbedded in the nature of the race. The instinct of assimilation is the first and foremost instinct in every living cell and it takes will power to restrict it when the means for gratifying it are at hand.

Digging Our Graves

"We dig our graves with our teeth" has often been said of us. Certain it is that we eat our way to our graves a long life never comes to the glutton, in fact the ***"longness"*** of your life is largely dependent on the ***"shortness"*** of your food supply 🙠🙡

It is now an accepted theory that many of our diseases arise from putrefaction of protein in the colon. Meat carries a large amount of protein and contains other elements which decompose quickly ❧❧

What Is Meat Really?

Stop and think what begins to happen to an animal the instant it is killed. It begins to putrefy, does not it? All meat, therefore, is nothing more nor less than decaying animal matter and as such forms debris which is expunged from the system at great expense of energy.

Scientists show us the proof that man was not originally a carnivorous (flesh-eating) animal. Man lived on fruits, nuts, grains and vegetables for the first few millions of years that he inhabited the globe. Proof of this is seen in the length of his colon and the nature of his teeth.

Dogs and all flesh-eating creatures are created with the short colon adapted to the rapid expulsion of poison from the system. They also have the fang-like, deep-rooted teeth necessary for biting and chewing meat.

The human colon is very long, thus necessitating much roughage in the diet. If much meat and other concentrated foods are eaten, to the exclusion of fibrous foods, their poisons, instead of being expelled, bank up in the colon, causing various ailments ❧❧

A Favorite Fallacy

You may say you "need meat to keep up your strength." ❧❧

Look at the horse. He is the strongest animal known, for his weight and size. He has done more of the world's hard work than all men and all other animals combined. Yet he lives exclusively on "greens," fodder and cereals.

Overeating is an expensive pleasure, and an even greater expense to your body than to your purse. In addition to the diseases it brings, it steals your energy. It saps your enthusiasm. It makes you a slow mover and a slow thinker. It makes you lazy mentally and physically. Every ounce of food over the amount necessary to the upkeep of the body is a drain on the entire system.

Brain Work vs. Stomach Work

The "sleepiness" you feel after a heavy meal is only your brain's inability to "think" because when your stomach has that big load to dispose of it sends out emergency calls to other parts of the body for their "reserves" of blood. Your head, being one of the extremities, is one of the first to respond to the call.

Your brain and stomach can't work at the same time. When your stomach is digesting meat and potatoes your brain won't digest ideas.

Those who have brain work to do in the afternoons should eat light lunches.

All public speakers have learned that they must eat a light evening meal, or preferably no food at all for several hours prior to appearing before an audience. Many a "heavy speech" is caused by a "heavy dinner."

The First Food Scientist

The greatest food scientist of the world was born in Italy in the fifteenth century. His name was Luigi Cornaro. At 40 his physicians gave him up to die.

But he was determined to cheat Death and began to study life scientifically. He discovered that the stomach was the crucial point, and he controlled his fate by controlling his stomach. He lengthened his life to 103 years, more than sixty happy, successful years over the allotted time.

He did it by eating very sparingly. Twelve ounces of solid food and fourteen ounces of unfermented fruit juice were all he allowed himself per day.

Every few months he went on a fast of several days—gave his stomach a chance to rest for a new start—and wrote best during these days when he had no food whatever.

Your "Alimentary" Age

Metchnikoff, the renowned French scientist, declared that 95 per cent of all human diseases come from putrefaction in the alimentary canal; that it is the "breeding ground" for most of our troubles.

E. E. Rittenhouse, Commissioner of Conservation for the Equitable Life Assurance Society, said in a speech at the Hotel Astor, New York: "The average American would not think of mixing bricks, scrap-iron or gravel with the fuel for his furnace, yet he feeds his stomach with tasty junk, much of which cannot be digested. This seriously overstrains his heart, arteries, kidneys, nerves and digestion."

Clogging Your Grate

The body may well be compared to a stove with the stomach as the firebox. The fire creates the heat and energy, which is exactly what the digestion of food does for your body.

But when you stoke your stomach with three or four big meals each day the same thing happens that happens in any stove—the ashes and clinkers accumulate in the form of various poisons and clog the grate.

The marvel of it all is that the human body stands so much neglect and abuse. Your body is the most intricate and wonderfully complex machine in the world and yet you expect it to run itself.

Colleges and Colons

Horace Mann said: "In college I was taught all about the motions of the planets as carefully as though they were in danger of flying off the track if I did not know how to trace their orbits; but nothing about the organization of my own body. Nothing could be more preposterous. I should have begun at home and taken the stars when it came their turn."

Your Toy Balloon

It is remarkable what wrong ideas people have on the subject of eating.

For one thing, few people know that the stomach is a flexible organ, somewhat like a small balloon, which can be distended or contracted as you choose. If you eat small amounts of food it becomes smaller and is satisfied with less. If you eat large amounts of food it distends until only large quantities satisfy it. It is like people—the more you give it the more it demands.

Here is a strange and little known fact about your stomach: The feeling of satisfaction of having "had all you want" comes from the fact that food is stretching the walls of the stomach.

When you have given your stomach a chance to become smaller, a smaller quantity of food gives this satisfied feeling. This is also the reason why you don't want as large a meal, after decreasing the diet a few days, as you used to require.

Right and Wrong Eating

Just as wrong eating is the cause of most of our ills, so correct eating will create and maintain bodily vigor and mental energy.

By right eating we do not mean freak diets- we mean just good, everyday foods properly combined 🙖🙖

Poor Food Combinations

Milk and sugar.
Fruits with coarse vegetables.
Acid fruits with starches.
Too many kinds of food at one meal.

Good Food Combinations

Fruits with cereals and nuts.
Nuts with all foods.
Vegetables with cereals and nuts.
Cereals with all other foods.
Milk with cereals.
Eggs with all other foods.

The Best Foods to Select From

Protein	*Fats*	*Carbohydrates*
Peas	Ripe Olives	Cereal
Beans	Olive oil	Fruits
Nuts	Cream	Sugar
Eggs and milk	Butter	Root vegetables
Cheese		Coarse "fodder"
Gluten products		vegetables

Include some from each class in each meal.

In weight eat one-tenth protein, one-tenth fats and eight-tenths carbohydrates.

Preferences May Be Poisons

What you like is not a safe guide. Do not, for the sake of tickling your palate for a few minutes, load your stomach with harmful foods that cost you hours of inefficiency and suffering.

Do not eat between meals. Your stomach needs a rest the same as all other organs.

Never eat when you are not hungry. A lack of hunger is your stomach's way of telling you that it is not ready for more food. Hunger is its signal that it is ready to digest food.

But it is not a signal that it is ready to digest a ton of junk.

Overweight and Underweight

The statistics of the U. S. insurance companies show that for each pound above normal you increase your chances of death one per cent above normal if disease strikes you.

The life insurance business, of stupendous proportions financially and industrially, is based on just one thing—the law of averages as applied to the length of your life.

To run a winning instead of a losing business on this guess, the insurance companies had to know what it was that made you "an unsafe risk."

They have discovered that fat is the thing that does it. They have found in the statistics compiled upon millions of Americans, that the fat man dies younger than the slender man.

The man whom you call "fat and husky" is much more likely to "drop off," so say the insurance companies, than the "skinny" man you sympathize with.

Fat and Your Ford Engine

An excess of fat overtaxes the heart. Your heart weighs less than a pound. It is the one organ that never takes a rest. There is that faithful little engine, thumping away every instant from the moment you are born till the moment you are dead.

If you live forty years that little engine has chugged away without an instant's cessation for forty years. If you live to be ninety it has chugged away for ninety years. Every other organ has rest periods, takes little vacations at night, in relaxed moments, etc. But not your heart.

Because it is such a little engine we will compare it to a Ford engine. Now a Ford engine is large enough for a Ford car, for Ford cars are light weight. As long as you do not weigh too much your engine will do the same for you. It will take you up the hills and down the dales of life at a pretty good gait.

But when you take on fat you are doing to your heart just what a Ford owner does to his engine when he loads the tonneau down with bricks.

A Ford engine will stand for a good many pounds of excess baggage, just as will your heart, but if you load in too much and attempt to carry it all the time, your car will not be in good running order very long.

You will not notice it at first. Along the paved streets of perfect health you will travel without anything going desperately wrong. You do your work, you jog along fairly satisfactorily, keeping up with the procession without apparent strain.

But come to a hill such as Pneumonia and Diabetes and the little engine fails to make the grade.

Thousands of men and women every year literally "kill their engines" just that way when they might so easily have had a long and happy life.

Fattening at Forty

Overweight is an infallible indication (except in dropsy) of overeating.

It is a false idea that you "just naturally fatten up after forty." Slower movements, less exercise, "the comforts of life,"—including richer food and more of it—are what fatten the middle aged man ❧❧

There is no reason why a man should weigh more at fifty than at thirty.

Following is the table of normal weights for men and women according to the U.S. insurance statistics:

Age 30—Men

Height Ft. In.	Pounds	Height Ft. In.	Pounds	Height Ft. In.	Pounds
5 0	126	5 7	148	6 1	178
5 1	128	5 8	152	6 2	184
5 2	130	5 9	156	6 3	190
5 3	133	5 10	161	6 4	196
5 4	136	5 11	166	6 5	201
5 5	140	6 0	172		
5 6	144				

Age 30—Women

Height Ft. In.	Pounds	Height Ft. In.	Pounds	Height Ft. In.	Pounds
4 8	112	5 2	124	5 8	146
4 9	114	5 3	127	5 9	150
4 10	116	5 4	131	5 10	154
4 11	118	5 5	134	5 11	157
5 0	120	5 6	138	6 0	161
5 1	122	5 7	142		

This table is for people of thirty years or over.

If you are under twenty your weight may be over or under without danger. If you are between twenty and thirty your weight may vary as much as five pounds under or five pounds over this table.

Fat Slows Down the Mind

Fat is a handicap in many ways. It decreases not only the quantity of life but the quality.

The individual who is much overweight finds not only his body less active but his mind also. He requires more sleep and requires it oftener than the man of normal weight. He is not as keen, dynamic or alert as he would be were he rid of his excess baggage.

Hundreds of our students have told us how much more alive were their minds, how much more happy and optimistic their mental condition after reducing ❧❧

Those who are overweight should first cut down the **quantity** of food.

Overweight and Overeating

No matter how little you are eating if you are overweight you are overeating. When a fat man declares to us that he eats but one head of lettuce a day, we say "cut the head in two."

As a matter of fact, the fat man or woman always overeats. The very presence of fat indicates the same thing that water does when it runs over—the pan is too full. Fat is merely the margin, the surplus, manufactured by the assimilative system, over and above the needs of the body.

If You Are Overweight

Avoid	*Eat*
White bread	Lettuce
Corn	Spinach
Rice	Carrots

<table>
<tr><td>Potatoes</td><td>Turnips</td></tr>
<tr><td>Olive oil</td><td>Cabbage</td></tr>
<tr><td>Butter</td><td>Onions</td></tr>
<tr><td>Cream</td><td>Radishes</td></tr>
<tr><td>Sugar in all forms</td><td>Celery</td></tr>
<tr><td>Pastry</td><td>Tomatoes</td></tr>
<tr><td>Fats of all meats</td><td>Green peppers</td></tr>
<tr><td>Custard</td><td>Bran bread or</td></tr>
<tr><td>Desserts of all kinds</td><td>Gluten bread</td></tr>
<tr><td></td><td>All fruits except
    bananas and grapes</td></tr>
</table>

If underweight reverse these lists.

Underweight, unless more than ten pounds, is not dangerous. Do not eat meat more than once a day. This applies to all persons regardless of weight ☙☙

Constipation

If inclined to constipation eliminate meat. Eat the "fodder" vegetables such as lettuce, spinach, celery, tomatoes, turnips, etc., and plenty of raw fruits.

Laxatives of any kind are dangerous; they tend to do the work belonging to the muscles of the colon, and these muscles, being relieved of their duties, ultimately become flabby and refuse to work.

Those who adhere to these rules and eat plenty of bran bread can cure themselves permanently of constipation.

What to Drink

Tea and coffee are harmful in proportion to the amount and the strength of same. Both tend to cause constipation. Neither should be taken more than once a day and then not strong.

All stimulants are dangerous. There are tea drunkards as well as whiskey drunkards.

Because water is, next to air, the most necessary food, you should drink at least eight glasses every twenty-four hours. It not only carries great food values of its own, but acts as a flush for poisons.

Two glasses of tepid water before breakfast are especially recommended for those who are troubled by constipation.

Biliousness

Biliousness is largely the result of constipation or of a lazy liver. The liver is the body's poison destroyer—the "garbage crematory" of the system—and when it fails to do its work the blood is flooded with poisons. This in turn causes brain fag as well as body fag. A torpid liver always makes a torpid mind.

To overcome a tendency to biliousness avoid sweets and starches and eat raw fruits.

Headaches

Most headaches come from constipation. The millions of microbes which inhabit the large intestine are often responsible for mental sluggish-ness and the "blues." When these poisons are too long retained in the colon and especially when they are greatly increased by overeating or too much meat in the diet, the increased production and absorption of poisons will cause headaches.

Headache remedies never cure your headache. They merely drug you into not feeling it. Instead of taking drugs clean out the intestines and colon

Your mind never works effectively when your body is working defectively. Many a giant intellect has been starved and eventually killed by the poisons absorbed from chronic constipation. Most supposedly "nervous" headaches are "constipation" headaches.

Rheumatism

Today it is known that rheumatism comes from infection somewhere in the system. Infection manufactures pus. When this pus has no outlet it is absorbed by the body. Rheumatism is the howl set up by your body when it has swallowed more of this poison than it can stand.

The source of the trouble may be anywhere in the body, but it has been found that the teeth and the tonsils are its favorite breeding grounds.

If you feel the warning twinges don't stop at the elimination of "red meats" or the indulgence in "frequent baths." Both measures are helpful, whether you are sick or well.

Have your teeth and tonsils "X-Rayed." The picture will probably reveal the tell-tale "black spots"—tiny abscesses that have been sending out their poisons, sometimes for years.

Dentistry is the infant among the sciences and has not yet devised methods for permanently crowning your decayed teeth successfully. There is always danger that the pretty exterior "covers a multitude of sins."

Sleeping

Your nerves resemble electrical batteries. Nerve energy is your electricity and the current is on during every waking moment.

Sleep is necessary for the recharging of these batteries

You may feel good for a long time on little sleep, but that is only because your nerves are "extending your credit." You can't borrow on the future indefinitely. The time is sure to come when they will foreclose.

Grief, joy, excitement, fear, anxiety—in fact, all emotional mental states— increase the voltage and run down your batteries. If you want health don't waste your electricity.

How Long Should I Sleep?

From six to eight hours of sleep are essential to the health of the average man and woman. Some require as much as nine while others keep well on an average of five hours of sleep.

No iron-clad rule can be laid down for all. Much depends upon the temperament of the individual. The only safe rule is this: Do not make a practice of sleeping less than five hours nor more than nine out of twenty-four.

Do not spend any more of your lifetime asleep than is necessary to good health but be sure to get all you need. This can be determined by noting carefully how you feel on the days after you have had the minimum of sleep.

In deciding whether lack of sleep is harmful to you, physical evidence alone is not sufficient. Watch your memory on the days following the minimum of sleep. This is the best test, for memory is the weakest link in your mental chain. You can safely estimate your "sleep capacity" in this manner.

Insomnia

Insomnia is not a disease but a symptom- an indication that something is wrong with you mentally or physically. Either your body is sick over something, or your mind is worried over something.

Many people think they have not slept when they really have. We are not conscious of sleep. We are only conscious of the intervals when we are awake.

Unless you have a watch beside your bed and time yourself you can never know how long you stayed awake in the night. The desire for sleep and the monotony always make your mind exaggerate the period of wakefulness.

Self-Deceived About Sleep

It has been found in hospitals and sanitaria where a nurse times the patient that he sleeps more than he thinks he does and the time that seems "hours" to him was only minutes, according to the clock.

This is the first step toward recovery—to realize that you are nine times out of ten getting more sleep than you imagine.

The second is this rather startling fact—which has been proven by scientists: It is not the loss of sleep that harms you so much as the worry over its loss ❧❧

A man lies awake a couple of hours in the night. He frets over it. He tells himself how badly he needs his rest and how miserable he is going to feel the next day. He gets all ready for a headache and when he awakens in the morning without one he says it will appear pretty soon.

He looks for it, expects it, mentally invites it, gets all ready for it and concentrates on it until he actually feels a headache coming on. But he, and not the sleeplessness, brought it.

How to Go to Sleep

Experiments have shown that one can lose a great deal of sleep without impairing the health, because when we do sleep we make up for the sleep lost by sleeping three or four times as soundly ❧❧

But worry is another matter. Worry at any time is dangerous to health. Therefore, when you find yourself wakeful remember the wakefulness won't harm you much but worry will.

Tell yourself that you are resting your body for the next day's demands. Relax every muscle. Relax your mind. Don't try to think or allow yourself to think intensely about anything.

Let your mind drift as if on a slow, smooth- flowing river. When it fastens itself on those worries or any other one subject detach it and set it floating again ❧❧

Sleep will usually come soon but if it does not, don't be discouraged. Take advantage of the opportunity to master yourself, and in a few nights you will be able to put yourself to sleep in this manner.

Causes of Sleeplessness

Most insomnia comes from letting your mind run wild. The above method for curing sleeplessness also cures you of the source of your trouble by giving mental discipline.

But remember, in this as in all things, your body and mind are interdependent. Aid your mind in following the above rules by avoiding all stimulants. You cannot key up your brain during the day by tea and coffee and expect it to subside at night.

You say you have to drink coffee to "brace you up." When you don't sleep you are merely braced up ❦❦

Sleep Before Midnight

Go to bed before midnight. If you are troubled by chronic insomnia, be in bed by ten o'clock.

It has been proved by scientific experiments that the period of greatest mental activity is between one and four in the morning. Many of the famous writers, including Herbert Spencer, reserved these hours for writing, declaring their keenest concentration and most brilliant thoughts came at that time.

Be sure to retire before this "wide-awake" period comes to you. The time varies somewhat with the individual. Watch yourself. Note the time when your natural "sleepy feeling" wears off and make a practice of retiring prior to it.

This wave of sleepiness will carry you safely into unconsciousness ❦❦

Then if you are careful to sleep in a quiet, well-ventilated room your chances for remaining asleep all night are good.

Spicy Foods Stimulate

Avoid rich or spicy foods just before retiring.

A glass of warm water, warm milk or broth will tend to draw the blood away from your head and induce sleep.

A tepid bath in which you lie completely relaxed for fifteen or twenty minutes just before going to bed is also excellent. Never take a hot or cold bath just before retiring, as both tend to stimulate heart action.

Sleep-Making Drugs

Never resort to sleep-producing drugs. They do not bring sleep but only distorted unconsciousness. Each dose decreases your tendency to natural sleep while increasing the necessity for a larger dose until, after using drugs, you find it impossible to fall asleep naturally.

In addition to these harmful results every drug of this kind is poisonous in itself.

The poisoning of the system in this way adds to your wakeful tendencies and thus you go around in a vicious circle. Better remain awake whole nights than contract the "sleeping-drug" habit.

Taking Troubles to Bed

The last warning for wakeful ones is this: Don't take your troubles to bed. They cannot be settled there. They only unsettle *you*. A well-known scientist has said: "Don't justify yourself by saying you only think things over. *Most thinking in bed is worry.*"

Relaxation

Man spends at least one-fourth of his life-time asleep. Thus the one who lives to 60 years has slept 15 years and the 80-year-old 20 years.

If you want to cut down these sleeping years remember this: When you are not doing anything else, relax. Let your muscles relax. Let your mind relax

Most people keep themselves tense and taut as a violin string from morning till night. Those who have insomnia get it by keeping themselves that way after they are in bed. This keeps the entire system so keyed up you are tired continually

In "High" All the Time

It is not your office work or housework that tires you so much as the hard work you make your muscles do between times.

You don't let go. You are geared "in high," as the autoists say. Your muscles are like so many soldiers. They are standing stiff and straight at "attention," ready for instant action.

This is part of the body's general plan of preparedness" and is maintained by a rapid succession of impulses raining down over every muscle of your body at the rate of about ten reflexes per second. The contraction is so rapid that it produces a sound somewhat like the vibration of a guitar string.

If you will put the tips of your fingers in your ears and then stiffen every muscle and hold them tense you can distinctly hear it.

It is estimated that at least 40 per cent of the energy expended daily by us is expended in this way and is equal to walking 20 miles or lifting a 5-pound weight 500 times.

This explains why worry and nervousness use up energy so rapidly.

"Loosen" Yourself

When you are in a state of high nervous tension you are burning up your strength at a rapid rate.

Avoid this destruction of your strength by relaxing as completely as possible whenever a moment's opportunity presents itself. Let yourself down whenever there is no necessity for strain. By doing this you will be ready with reserve strength when the emergencies arrive.

Whenever you are waiting for a car, an elevator, a clerk, waiter or any kind of service, remember they are doing it, not you, and take it as an opportunity to rest every fibre of your body. After the street car or elevator comes and you are started, relax again till your destination is reached, and give those tight muscles a little vacation. Do this for one day and see what it will do for you.

If you are in work where you can completely relax for five minutes each hour you will require 25 per cent less sleep and come to the end of each day much less weary. The efficiency of the nation's biggest men is maintained largely by this secret.

Only the one cylinder individual keeps chugging every instant. Relax!

Exercise

Motion is essential to the healthful condition of all animate things. Man's health depends more than we think on his muscular activity. But this does not necessarily mean strenuous exercise.

Whether or not intense physical activity is essential to health depends entirely upon the type of the individual.

A muscular man or woman that is, the type whose muscles are highly developed-requires strenuous muscular activity in order to stay well. He should take this kind of exercise. If his work does not provide it he should get it outside his work ♪♪

On the other hand, the very mental person whose chief ambition is to read a book, has less. Muscular development and requires less muscular activity ♪♪

Exercises For All

The safest law as to exercise is this: Three miles of walking in the open air every day for all types, with the following simple exercises the first thing in the morning and the last thing at night. They "tone up" the system.

1. Stand erect, with arms hanging at sides. Bend your body at the waist to the right, reaching down toward the floor as far as possible. Then bend your body to the left, trying to reach the floor with your left hand. Do this 10 times at first, gradually increasing to 40 times.

2. Stand erect. Place hands on hips. Twist your body to the right as far as possible without moving your feet, then twist your body as far to the left as possible. This is one of the best liver exercises. Do 10 times at first, increasing to 50.

3. Lie flat on your back. Fold your arms. Raise both legs together to a perpendicular position. Then lower them together slowly. Begin with 5 and increase to 20 times. This is the best stomach exercises 🙠🙠

4. Lie flat on your back. Fold your arms. Slowly raise yourself to a sitting position, then slowly lower yourself again to a reclining position. Begin with 5 times and increase to 20.

5. If you have but little opportunity for walking you can exercise your feet and ankles by this exercise: Stand erect with feet almost touching. Slowly raise yourself up and down on your toes. Stand firmly. Start with 10 times and increase to 25.

6. If you spend much time indoors give yourself the following lung exercises at an open window several times a day: Lift your chest, draw in deep breaths, filling the lungs to full capacity. Then slowly expel the air. Force the air deep down into the very lowest portion of your lungs, and expel all of it before taking the next breath

Dumb Bell Exercises

(Women should use bells weighing from 2 to 4 pounds each and men from 4 to 6 pounds.)

1. Stand erect. Raise arms straight up, then lower straight in front of you until they are at right angles with the body. Raise and lower 5 times, increasing to 10.

2. Raise arms straight up. Lower the right arm down the right side and the left arm down the left side until they are at right angles with the body. Raise and lower from 5 to 10 times.

3. Stretch both arms straight out in front of you. Then swing back and forth horizontally. Start with 10 and increase to 20 times. This is the best exercise for taking fat off the shoulder blades and for putting muscle on them

4. Hold right arm straight out at right side. Then swing it from back to front in a circle as wide as possible. Do the same with the left arm. This strengthens the shoulders and removes surplus flesh. Start with 10 and increase to 20 times for each.

5. Hold arms straight out in front of you. Then swing them as high as possible and as low as possible in a semi-circle. Start with 10 times and increase to 20.

Outdoor exercises may be according to the preferences of the individual. Nature is wiser than we. If outdoor exercise is necessary to the upkeep of your particular system you will know about it through your wireless—your natural inclinations

Hints For Each Type

To reduce, fat people need not resort to the violent exercises sometimes recommended, but should do so by reversing the condition which caused overweight, i.e., by decreasing the quantity of food. They may participate in whatever outdoor recreations are preferred.

It is impossible to separate mental and physical reactions. When the mind does not like what the body is doing the maximum of physical benefit is not possible.

Florid people should take part in exercises and sports requiring short spurts of energy, preferably baseball, tennis and other diversions sufficiently keen to meet the requirements of their enthusiastic nature.

Those of extreme muscular development enjoy and thrive upon the most strenuous physical activities, such as racing, running, football, etc.

Those men and women who are tall, angular, "raw-boned,"— who have a larger proportion of bone in the body structure than the average—usually care only for such recreations as hiking, golf, and exercises calling for slow movements over long distances.

The undersized, dreaming, reading individual who dislikes all forms of physical exertion, can remain surprisingly well without exercise but even he should walk his three miles a day.

Don't Forget to Walk!

The brain never works so well as when one is walking in the open air. Walking is a brain stimulant. The reason for this is that clear thinking is only accomplished when the blood is circulating fairly rapidly through the brain. Walking speeds up heart action. In other words, it does for you just what the cup of black coffee does, but without its penalties.

How We Keep Well

Keeping in health is largely a matter of ripening the new cells and expelling the old ones. The body is composed of billions of cells and these cells are of three kinds or stages-those just ripening, those in their prime and those that are dying

Keeping well is largely a matter of keeping this evolutionary process speeded up to the point where new cells are not retarded in their growth nor dead ones retained.

Walking and other forms of exercise are valuable as a preventative of the clogging-up. Disease is nothing but this clogging-up carried to the danger point.

Watch Your Thinking!

No lesson on health in these enlightened days can be completed without this warning: Your thinking vitally affects your health. Worry, fear, anxiety—all negative moods—tear down millions of cells each moment and at the same time tend so to obstruct the normal functioning of the body that these cells, which have turned into debris, are not carried away.

No man of unhealthy thoughts can have a healthy body. If you would be sure of a strong body keep a sharp eye on the thoughts that you permit to take possession of your brain.

Interrelation of Body and Brain

For centuries it has been acknowledged that the mind influences the body. We know that mental disorders sometimes produce physical diseases.

We know that any kind of mental disturbance decreases physical vitality. An unpleasant story can cause nausea. The keenest hunger disappears when you receive a telegram bearing sad news. On the other hand the body also influences the mind. Lesions in the brain cause insanity and other mental disorders.

Another evidence of the body's influence on the mind is seen in the following: Whenever you are physically tired your memory is not up to par. A cup of black coffee put into your stomach speeds up your mental activities.

As a matter of fact, your body and your brain are married and they will never be divorced. What affects one affects the other.

Your Freight System

Man is a unit; he is a marvelously organized community of millions of cells. Each little cell is a distinct and separate being with a work and a life of its own. The health and happiness of each cell or group of cells affects all other cells composing the commonwealth of the body. The feelings of each group of cells—those of the liver, lungs, brain and other organs—instantly affect the feelings of all other groups.

This is done by means of your circulatory system (the blood vessels) and your nervous system (your nerves). Your circulatory system—from the big trunk lines of the arteries down to the tiniest blood vessels—carries the different chemicals necessary for the upkeep of the body, just as a freight train carries many kinds of commodities to many stations.

Your Telegraph System

Your nervous system is the most perfect telegraph system in the world. Over its wires is flashed the news of every thought, sound, taste, touch, odor and sight that comes within the range of your senses.

When any of these senses encounters an unpleasant or destructive experience the message of it is instantly sent out to your circulatory system and injects into the blood the harmful chemicals known as toxins.

When something pleasant, beautiful or joyous happens to these senses the news flashed over the wires creates life-giving chemicals in the blood stream ❧❧

Any part of the body thus instantaneously influences every other part for good or ill through the medium of these intricately interwoven systems ❦❦

Every cell is equipped with a tiny nerve of its own and keeps in constant touch with everything that is going on in the rest of the body.

Your "Mental Messages"

When a single group of cells can thus influence all other groups think how much more powerful is the influence of the whole mind.

The mind presides over the very citadel of the nervous system. It handles all mental messages sent out by the nervous system and modifies the chemical freight carried by the circulatory system.

The potent factor in all mental healing is the removal of fear from the mind. It does not so much matter how this is accomplished—whether by faith, hope, argument, reason or even superstition ❦❦

The primitive Hawaiian, in the famous play, "The Bird of Paradise," dies because she believes the priest is praying her to death. The same superstition reversed would work the opposite result.

Faith and Fear

The different types of people in our own country respond to different types of belief concerning the question of mind control.

The religious-minded is impressed when it comes to him in the form of religion; the scientific- minded is convinced by the respective effects of fear and faith on the human body; the every-day practical man accepts it when he sees the different physical conditions caused in him by joy and by sorrow.

Fear poisons the body. When this pall of fear is lifted a big step has been taken toward the cure.

Faith may not cure the body but it does stop the secretion of the fear poisons. This gives nature a chance to go on with her marvelous healing processes •••

When she stands ready to do these wonders for you don't you think the least you can do is to give her a chance? Stop shackling her with your fear thoughts. Give her a free rein.

If you cannot at first believe in the healing power of faith at least keep a serene neutrality. Pretty soon, when you see the wonders Nature performs in clearing up your troubles, you will realize that faith in her is justified.

Nature's Many Miracles

Maybe you do not believe in "miracles." But you witness one every time a cut on your finger heals up. You can't explain how it is done. It is something man cannot do for himself. But Nature does it. Her one idea is to keep you well. She never for a moment relaxes her vigil over you.

No matter how material-minded you are, you can't get around the fact that any force which turns your sickness into health deserves your co-operation at least.

Physical and Psychological Necessities

The first step is to supply the material necessities of life—right breathing, right eating, right exercising, right drinking, right sleeping.

The second is to supply the right thoughts—stimulating, optimistic, courageous thoughts, for thoughts vitally affect your physical condition and the length of your life.

Since your mental attitude affects your physical condition, avoid the subject of disease. Avoid talking, reading or thinking about abnormal conditions of the human body. Above all, do not look for symptoms within yourself of any disease.

Our parting word to you is: Stop worrying. Keep your mind full of uplifting, vitalizing thoughts. In the next lesson we will tell you how to do this.

LESSON V

How to Stay Young

*"The minute a man ceases to improve,
no matter what his years, that minute
he begins to be old."*

—William James

IN the past people went to two extremes in their ideas concerning the prolongation of youth. There were those who foolishly believed in "charms" and miracles for restoring lost youth ⁂⁂

As children we all learned in our histories of the expedition of Ponce de Leon, who claimed to have discovered the "Fountain of Eternal Youth" on the Western hemisphere, and of the pilgrimages of those who believed him.

To the other extreme have gone those who took it for granted that the prolongation of youth or youthfulness beyond a certain arbitrary point was impossible.

Neither of these extremes is right.

Today all thinking people recognize the possibility of extending the period of youthfulness far into the years of later life, and the methods for doing so are in practice.

It is these means and methods which we are going to give you in this lesson.

A Biological Law

If the idea of extending life and prolonging youth seems fantastical to you, turn to the laws of nature, to your biology. There you will find that in all mammals except man the period of life is *five times the period of growth.* A dog gets its full growth in two years and lives ten; a horse in five years and lives twenty-five.

Man, who does not attain his full physical stature until twenty, nor physical development before twenty-five, should therefore live from **one hundred to one hundred and twenty-five years,** normally ✤✤

Making The Same Mistakes

One of the greatest tragedies in life is that just as we learn how to live we die. Just as we have learned the value of life it is taken away.

When the great men and women have proven their right to lead us and gained our confidence, they pass on. And each generation makes all over again most of the mistakes of previous generations! ✤✤

All great men and women leave their work unfinished. Susan B. Anthony, the great founder of the Woman's Suffrage Movement in America, said on her death-bed at eighty-six, "I have done so little."

The gain to the world when we learn how to keep youth cannot be measured. Even these great people who did so much for us could have accomplished more had they realized the possibility of extending the period of their service.

Work To the End

That it is possible to do this has been proved. Titian painted up to the time of his death at ninety-nine ✤✤

La Place, the astronomer, made one of his greatest discoveries just before his death, at eighty-eight.

Gladstone was Prime Minister of England at eighty-three, and the year before mastered a new language.

Rodin, the greatest sculptor of modern times, died at seventy-seven, and produced some of his greatest masterpieces in the last months of his life.

William Dean Howells, who reached nearly ninety, had not only a young body but a mind so young that he was to the day of his death in charge of a department, "The Easy Chair," in one of America's leading magazines.

Ella Wheeler Wilcox and Amelia E. Barr wrote brilliantly up to their last days, though advanced in ears far beyond the supposed "limit" of three score and ten. Sarah Bernhardt, at 76, held the laurels as the world's greatest actress.

All of these obeyed, consciously or unconsciously, most of the laws laid down in this lesson.

If you will obey them, you can add from five to fifty years to your life.

What Makes Us Old?

Before we tell you these rules let us see what it is that makes people old. The processes are both mental and physical as are all processes of thinking creatures ❧❧

The mistakes people make concerning their bodies are manifold. If you want to keep your body young, obey the rules on "How To Be Well" as given in the preceding lesson.

In this chapter we shall explain the part that the mind both conscious and subconscious plays in the aging of an individual.

Age and the Subconscious

As we have already seen, the 90 per cent of the mind which is subconscious forms the main-spring of our conduct.

You think and act, not in accordance with your reason, as you fondly suppose, but more or less automatically in response to the habits of this submerged nine-tenths of your mind.

Yours may be likened to the cargo of an ocean liner which lies out of sight.

The most important part of it is under the surface. The direction in which you go, the port at which you arrive, depend on how the machinery works down there in the hull.

Suggestion and Age

As we have already found, the subconscious is made largely by suggestion. It takes on its tendencies from suggestion, and in accordance with these suggestions directs your life.

How does this affect youthfulness?

From early babyhood we are taught that we will grow old at a certain time.

We are informed when we ask why other people have gray hair, stooped shoulders and wrinkles, that these things are the result of age.

When we ask what is meant by age we are told that all people at forty or so begin to look like that. We are told that when we have lived forty years or more we too will begin to look like that ❧❧

The certainty of it sinks into our minds, and from that day we *invite, expect* and *prepare* for old age.

"After Forty"

We think of the years up to forty as the only years in which we can accomplish. We think of everything after that as a general fading-out.

We consider ourselves of middle age at fifty and expect nothing of ourselves after sixty.

The parents who have property decide early in life how they are going to divide it among their children. They get ready to relinquish it.

Father, who is as good a man as any of his sons, divides the farm or the business; mother passes her pretty things—the real lace, her jewelry and other treasures—on to her daughters, saying, "I shall not need them anymore. I am getting too old for them. I will not live to wear them out."

They make all preparations, save those of the undertaker, for laying themselves on the shelf.

If they do not have property, they wonder which of their children they will inflict themselves upon when they are old.

They have gone along to a certain age—the age when people are **supposed** to grow old—and they think it is time to droop, time to sag, time to begin the process of decay.

They resign themselves to it, talk about it, think about it, write to their friends about it, and look for it in others.

"Am I Older?"

The first question a woman usually asks of another woman after she passes her thirtieth milestone is, "Don't you think I am looking older? Tell me honestly, now!"

Men don't ask it of their friends, but they would if they dared.

Pretty soon they walk, talk, sag, droop and act like old men and women. The man who walks, talks, sags and thinks like an old man is soon in very truth an old man.

They keep themselves reminded of their advancing years. They are conscious of every moment of their age. They call attention to the fact that they are getting old by having birthday parties which remind not only themselves but all others of "how time is flying."

Father watches the mirror for baldness and mother for double chins. They say they must not spend this or that because they are going to need it for their "old age." They do not attempt new projects because they fear they will not be able to finish them.

We Limit Our Lives

This feeling that one's time is limited is responsible for the loss to the world of many great achievements ❧❧

A psychologist whose knowledge and accuracy could not be doubted, once said, "consciousness of the passage of time has a great influence in printing wrinkles in our faces and graying our hairs."

In substantiation of it he told a story, for whose authenticity we cannot vouch, but out of which we will ask you to take the grain of philosophy it contains.

Story of a Girl

The story goes that a beautiful girl of twenty years was engaged to be married. At the hour for which her wedding had been set and just as she was dressed for the ceremony, word was brought that her fiancé had been killed.

The shock robbed her of her reason. She never regained it, though she lived to be 81 years old. Every day of her life thereafter she dressed herself in her trousseau at the wedding hour and waited for her bridegroom.

The wedding gown turned yellow with age. The veil became tattered shreds, but the face of the woman remained that of a twenty-year-old girl. Her hair did not turn gray. The plumpness of her cheeks was but slightly diminished and her form was as girlish as it had been sixty years before.

The writer who vouched for the story declared he believed the retention of her youth was due to the fact that she had *no consciousness of the passage of time.*

To her, she was always twenty years old.

Every day was her wedding day.

This story may or may not be true, but there is a good suggestion in it nevertheless.

Some Self-Tests

If you want to know whether or not you are making yourself old ahead of your time try these tests on yourself:

Are you living in the past?

Do you think of the times that are gone as the best times? ❧❧

Do you live over the triumphs and successes of the past?

Do you give more thought to remembering the successes of yesterday than to planning successes for the future?

Are you beginning to tell fibs about your age?

Are you habitually comparing yourself with younger people, regretting that you have lost your youthful charms?

Are you beginning to look for ill health?

Are you keeping an eagle eye out for the ***"break"*** in your physical condition?

Are you always wishing you could start over with the knowledge of today?

Are you constantly reminding yourself that there would be some chance for you if you could start all over five, ten or twenty years back, and are you taking it for granted that because you can't do this you cannot amount to anything?

Do you dislike to see the seasons roll around because each one ticks off a segment of your life?

Do you spend time resenting, hating, envying other people?

Are you in the habit of excusing yourself for not accomplishing as much as other people on the ground that you are older than they?

Are you getting careless about your personal appearance—the way you do your hair, the fit of your clothes—and slouching a bit in your walk? ❧❧

Do you say, just because a garment is of light color, "Oh that is too young for me?"

If you are doing these things you are beginning to slide down the grade to old age.

Danger Signals

If you are getting habitual about anything, if you are getting "set" in your ways, less open minded—if you find it hard to laugh at things that are really funny, you are making yourself old.

If you are doing things just as you have done them for years in spite of all our modern inventions and better methods, you are getting old.

If you dislike to make new friends, you are getting old ❧❧

If you think you have to do anything *just because you always have done it*, you are getting old ❧❧

If you can't have your plans upset without feeling that the world is in a jumble, you are getting old ❧❧

If you can only do certain things on certain days, or under certain conditions, you're getting old ❧❧

If you are voting the same old ticket your father voted, without knowing why, you are getting old. If you are voting the Republican ticket because you didn't approve of Bryan's 16 to 1 ideas, you are getting old. If you are voting the Democratic ticket for no other reason than that you happen to believe in the free coinage of silver, you are equally out of date.

If you call all Socialists "anarchists," and all radicals "alien enemies," you are forty years behind on the first conviction and already five years behind on the second. Catch up with the procession! ❧❧

If you are still going every Sunday to the same old church for the same old reasons that led you to affiliate with it thirty years ago, *without investigating whether or not it is meeting the soul needs of people*, you are getting old.

If you can't understand why anybody else should belong to a different church or a different party from yours, you are getting old.

If you can't get enthusiastic about anything to the point where you are just *a little bit crazy about it,* you are getting old.

If you have n't had a real thrill over something within the last six months, if you have not been thoroughly aroused for something, against something, by something or despite something, you are getting old

If you have not changed your mind about some fairly big world question during the last ten history-making years, you are getting old. ✺✺

If you have not laughed till the tears came to your eyes several times in the last year, you are getting old. If you have not felt those same tears spring to your eyes lately at the sight of suffering, you are getting old.

If your children make engagements to go out in the evening saying, "I'll get mother to come over and take care of the babies," without asking your permission, you are getting old.

If you turn up your nose at psychology; if you deplore the movies; if you declare that the successful acting of tragedy died with Mansfield and comedy with Nat Goodwin, you are getting old ✺✺

And here is the last and perhaps the crucial test: Do you look with impatience, sarcasm or superiority on the activities, foibles and madness's of young people?

If you take a "holier than thou" attitude whenever you see two young things spooning in the park and mutter, "There's one born every minute," you are getting old and you are getting there fast, and incidentally hastening the minute when *your* place will be taken by one of them. But take this consolation—you are not hopeless.

Nature is Simple

The ways to stay young are simple ways—ways so simple that we are inclined to underestimate them ❧❧

The ways for staying young are Nature's ways and therefore normal and easy of comprehension ❧❧

But man has always, in seeking the solution to a vital problem, looked far off when the real answer usually lay at his very feet—like the man who wandered around the world in search of a four-leaf clover and when he came home to die, discovered one growing *at his own doorstep.*

To Stay Young

First of all, if you would stay young, lure out, reason out or blast out of your subconscious mind the notion that you have just naturally got to wither and die when you have lived a certain number of years on this earth. Do you know that at no time are you more than two years old?

Not a cell in your body is two years old. The body and the brain are in a constant state of building up and tearing down, of creating and casting off cells, and the oldest cell in your body at this moment has not been there more than 18 months ❧❧

Today you do not have in your lungs one cell that was there four months ago.

Your Changing Cells

People get old because they imagine the material of which they are made gets old like cloth.

The difference between you and the piece of cloth is that you are constantly changing.

The stuff you are made of is *alive. Twenty million* red globules are manufactured in your blood every time you breathe.

The new cells, as they ripen, take on the shape and attitude of those they are succeeding, and each is so deeply impressed by the subconscious with the feeling of age that to all outward appearances it is an old cell.

What Edison Says

If this sounds unscientific let us refer you to an even more advanced statement in defense of it by the most scientific man of our time—Thomas A. Edison. This is Mr. Edison's theory and he carries it so far as to declare, ***"Every cell in us thinks."***

In the place of your old delusion that you must die after a certain number of years, charge your subconscious with the realization of the ever changing materials of which your body and brain are made

We do not say that this will enable you to live forever, but we do know that it will tend to make every cell take on the youth-attitude instead of the age-attitude.

We do know that those men and women who have lived longest *all* had this attitude of mind.

Decide on a Century

Let yourself realize that you are entitled, according to the laws of biology, to from one hundred to one hundred and twenty-five years of life the same as all other mammals.

Stop looking for the signs of age. ***We always find what we look for.***

Stop worrying about getting old. As we found in a previous lesson, worry tends to ***bring about what you worry about.***

It is more true in connection with old age than almost any other one thing, for the reason that all worry brings wrinkles, negative processes and ill health.

Every fear thought tears down tissue and that dead tissue becomes debris. Also, all worry thoughts slow up the improving processes to such an extent that you never quite catch up again.

Worry Brings Age

But worry about old age is more disastrous in bringing old age than any other worry for the scientific reason which we have noted before and which is known to all physiologists and psychologists—that every ***thought*** has its ***corresponding muscular mechanism.*** That mechanism reacts with every thought.

Whenever you worry about wrinkles, wrinkles respond. Whenever you are sad, the corners of your mouth go down. When you are happy those same corners turn up.

Unlock Your Mind

Read two newspapers. If you have long been a subscriber to the most conservative sheet in your neck of the woods, give yourself a chance to know the other side by taking a radical one.

The same holds good if the most radical paper is all you have been seeing for the last five years.

Unlock your mind. No matter how rusty the key it will work, for remember, you are ***not quite dead*** ❦❦

In addition to these, take the best magazines. If you feel you can't afford to, cut down on your food and save the money that way.

Inasmuch as the chances are that you are eating twice the amount you ought to for longevity, you will be killing two birds with one stone.

Don't Live in the Past

Don't talk of the past.

Talk of the future.

Think of the future.

Work for the future.

Believe there *is* a future for you.

You are justified in believing this because believing it will make you act in such a way as to live longer and *make* a future for yourself.

Eliminate Birthdays

Never let anyone have another birthday party for you. If that is the best hint you can think of for getting presents out of your friends, let them go.

Stop telling your age.

Forget right now how old you are and never allow yourself to think of it again.

Refuse to talk age or let others talk it to you.

Degenerating into Nursemaid

Don't let your children think you have so little to do in your own life that you can be called upon at any time to act as nursemaid to the grand-children. ❧❧

Get some engagements of your own. Get some evening engagements.

Do not begin to divide your property. Make a will if you have any property and then forget it.

Dress and Age

Don't dress in dull colors and things bespeaking age ❧❧

The reason for this is that we are all ***powerfully influenced by our garments.***

We always tend to act the role for which we are dressed. We play the part that goes with the costume ❧❧

If you do not believe it, recall that time you went to the masquerade as "Cap-and-Bells," "The Spanish Dancer," "Mephisto" or "The Colonial Maiden." Will you ever forget how you almost *felt* yourself the character for which you were dressed?

We do not recommend that every woman, regardless of her age or complexion, wear cerise, turquoise blue or paddy green. But no woman, however old, should wear dark colors exclusively.

At ninety, pastel shades, lavenders, palest pinks, yellows and white are more becoming than any somber shade.

These are the colors of youth, of spring, of freshness. In them you feel younger, and when you feel younger you are younger.

When you are in drab colors you feel drab and act drab.

Don't Forget Your Hair

Take pains with your hair. If you are a man don't get careless about the crease in your trousers ❧❧

If you are a woman, guard against that dumpy, matronly figure ❧❧

Keep Your Mind Alive

Regardless of sex inquire into your own mind, find out why you believe as you do on the questions of the day.

If there are big, vital questions concerning which you have no opinion whatever, investigate the merits and get one.

Enjoy Young People

Take an interest not only in your own children, but in other people's children. Cultivate their friendship ❧❧

This does not mean being kittenish—it means sympathizing with their viewpoints, hopes and ambitions ❧❧

Start New Things

Attempt new things with the determination that you are certainly going to win, and you will be surprised to see how easily they can be accomplished.

Start new projects with the firm conviction that even though they take ten or twenty years you will live to finish them.

Never say, "It is too late for me to start this or that." Never say, "If I could have done that five years or ten years ago that would have been different, but it is too late now."

Begin Now

Stop bemoaning the fact that you can't begin all over at the beginning.

You can do that very thing if you will start today. The past years will merely stand you in hand with their harvests of experience.

The "Breakdown"

Refuse to look for or expect the "breakdowns" other people have.

Stop turning the microscope of your mind inward whenever you may happen to have a stitch in your side, a twinge in a muscle or a slight dizziness.

Love Somebody

Never think of yourself as old.

If you are unmarried find someone with whom you can fall in love. Whether it is reciprocated or not, it will stir up your liver and do you good ❦❦

If you are married, fall in love with your own partner again ❦❦

Make New Friends

Give yourselves some vacations. Take some trips, if only in the Ford, away from everybody who knows you, your past, your age and your ailments.

Make new friends and cultivate them.

In Harmony with Nature

Try to live in harmony with all Nature, from the elimination of anger and fear to a sympathy with the first meadow lark you hear in the spring. In other words, keep each of those millions of cells thoroughly alive.

Delay the Undertaker

Make up your mind to keep the undertaker waiting *just as long as possible.*

Keep abreast of the movements in your community, state and nation. Know something of what is going on everywhere, from the little house next door to the Russian Revolutions.

Look Outward

Get out of yourself. All those who have lived to a great age were unselfish, outgiving natures who were interested in others.

We asked Mary C. C. Bradford, when she was president of the National Education Association, how she kept, through her strenuous professional activities, her buoyant youthfulness.

"By keeping alive my interest in all big things," she said.

"What one thing would you say was most important to one who desired to perpetuate his youth?" we asked.

"To participate in as many worth-while public activities as possible," she answered.

Keep Busy

As is well known, any machine disintegrates with idleness. The old saying that "Rest is rust" is as true of the human machine as any other.

A perpetual renewing process is always going on within you. Physical and mental activities speed up this process.

Four Mental Attitudes

There are four mental states which produce age—the *serious* attitude, the *depressed* attitude, the *superficial* attitude and the *excited* attitude.

As depression slows down the renewing processes to the point where debris piles up, so excitement speeds up those processes till the belts fly off the wheels.

The superficial or frivolous attitude, if carried to an extreme, means that no matter how long you live you are never going to grow up.

On the other hand, the attitude of taking life too seriously makes you "a little old man" or "a little old woman" before your time.

Be Moderate

The cure of these age-producing attitudes is poise—self-control. Let yourself feel deeply, determine to live fully, but control yourself.

Moderation in all things has been the rule of all who achieved long life.

Vitality and Youth

Treasure your vitality. It is the secret of youth. Avoid everything that could dissipate it—over-eating, under-nourishment, idleness, too hard work, extremes of any kind.

Why We Haven't Known

"If youth could be retained, why is it," you ask, "that we have not been taught these things before?"

The answer is simple. We are never taught the most vital and necessary truths of life. We are taught about ancient wars when we ought to be finding out about food values.

We are taught algebra, calculus and other higher forms of mathematics which we never use and are left in ignorance of the body's effect on the mind and the mind's effect on the body.

We are taught languages though we may never get out of our own hometown.

We are taught how to conjugate verbs, and to differentiate between the penult and the antepenult, but are kept in the dark as to the deepest desires of our natures—the sex instinct, the craving for a mate, and love.

We are taught everything except what we need to know.

The impractical, theoretical and ethereal is put into the curriculum. The things we need to know to save us from terrors, tragedy, shame and failure are left out.

Every human being longs to stay young. Yet the simple, certain rules by which he could do so are never given to him. The world was a long time in formulating these rules because the law by which youth can be perpetuated is both physical and metaphysical.

Youth Is Natural

Many things stay young. Why not you?

Last summer we saw in the Redwood forests of California thousands of trees that had stood there since before Christ—trees that had seen the seasons come and go before Nero was born, that had waved their branches toward the Golden Gate before Cleopatra's time.

Is it unreasonable, in the face of such facts, to anticipate the time when man, the highest thinking creature, shall control to a great extent the length of his own existence? Why not?

Your New Organs

The average person who breathes deeply of fresh air gets three new pairs of lungs every year.

A stomach that is not overloaded nor abused renews itself at least twice a year. This is true of every other abdominal organ.

The skin is completely renewed every month; the heart, brain and nervous systems every ninety days ❧❧

Eternal Youth

When the law of perpetual renewal is not violated, when we think right, expect youth and live up to the laws of health, there is no knowing to what length man may not perpetuate his youth.

The Passage of Time

The feeling that we are growing old comes from the belief that we have that much less time in which to live, whereas science has proven that the *years do not produce age.*

The consciousness of age is therefore nothing more or less than a consciousness of the *passing of time* ❧❧

Old Age Abnormal

Conditions which have produced age are abnormal instead of natural, and can only be removed by the development of a new consciousness ❧❧

This new consciousness must be based upon the realization that what is true in nature's other processes is true of the human system.

Perpetual Renewal

The most important of these are the processes of perpetual renewal and of present creation.

The first rebuilds the entire human system during every ten or eleven months, thus keeping the body physically young.

The second process creates in the system all those conditions of which the mind is conscious.

When your mind is conscious of this second process you know that there is no other time in nature but the now. To live absolutely in the NOW is to be conscious only of what is true in the now, and it is true that every cell in man is momentarily being created

Habit-Thinking and Age

By living in the belief that we are growing older every year, man has given a standing order to his subconscious to keep him reminded of his advancing years, to make him look older and feel older every year.

Every person is doing this through the force of habit—race habit. He has been training his subconscious mind ***toward producing old age.***

All Is Changing

Nothing is fixed, nothing is the same today that it was yesterday. All is change, and the purpose of this change is to make all things new at all times.

Every force in nature is working to counteract old age. Every movement of every muscle has youth and progress in view.

Newer and Better Thinking

You must train your mind perpetually to renew itself. This may be promoted by training every process of thinking to form new thought, better thought, greater thought about everything.

Improve Each Time

That is why we urge you to keep up with the times

Today's thought on any subject should be new as compared to the thought of yesterday.

Every idea should be an improvement upon the corresponding idea of last week. Every conception formed by your mind today on any subject should be finer, higher and better than the previous conception ❧❧

Brain-Atrophy

People get old because they think "old thoughts"—the same thoughts they have thought for years. No new brain cells are vitalized under this procedure. No new association centers are organized. This means brain-atrophy.

Use Each Experience

Nature's workings do not produce the conditions of age. These conditions are produced by man's *refusal to lend himself* to the renewing processes of nature. People who have passed through experiences of many kinds consider themselves old and worn because we look upon experience as a wearing process instead of a renewing process.

To stay young, train your mind to use every experience, every association center, for the awakening of *more mental power.*

Enlarge Your Horizon

When we have trained ourselves to think of every experience as a developing, *enlarging* process we will no longer grow old from experience, but will rather capitalize it and let it teach us how to stay young.

Every experience tends to produce an impression on the mind. Whether that impression is aging or revivifying depends on the *mental attitude toward the experience* while the impression was being made.

"Passing Thru" Things

Simply to "pass through" an experience is to impress yourself with the idea of wear and tear, but to look on every experience as the gateway **to larger and larger growth** will tend to make that experience, no matter how intense it may be, leave development instead of decay.

An Open Mind

You must not allow yourself to settle into grooves.

Never permit yourself a final conclusion on anything. Always keep your mind open. No one has any right to final conclusions; everything is comparative, nothing is absolute.

The fixed ideas of most people are merely **thoughts gone to seed.** If you have prejudices your mind is ossified.

Working Against Yourself

To stay young is natural.

Every condition that is adverse to nature produces age. Whenever your body or your mind is not working with nature it is working against it

From the time a child first hears about old age his mind begins to work against nature, to take it for granted that he will look old, feel old and be old when he has had a certain number of birthdays

Mind and Body

When the interdependence of body and mind is better understood, when we have discovered more of nature's physical and mental laws, the average life of the individual will be several times what it is today.

Have An Aim

In order to prolong your own life let us give you this final word: Have an absorbing aim in life.

If there is something you want to do ***begin it today*** regardless of how many years have elapsed since you were born.

Expel from your mind the notion that there is a deadline at fifty, sixty, or even ninety. Don't give up your professional or financial ambition just because of your age.

Read the biographies of successful men and women and see how many of them made their fame and fortune after middle age.

About Mark Twain

Mark Twain was "dead broke" at sixty and owed more than one hundred thousand dollars. In the sixteen years which elapsed after that, before his death, he not only repaid every penny but left a large fortune.

Walt Mason, who writes the rippling rhymes you read every morning at breakfast, says: "At forty-three I was a jobless misfit."

For some time, he has been receiving twenty-five thousand dollars a year for doing the thing he always liked to do, but which he had never before been able to capitalize.

Stop Committing Suicide

You are never too old to start over. If you start at what you like to do, it alone will perpetuate your youth.

Seneca said, "Man does not die, he kills himself." ❧❧

LESSON VI

How to Build Will Power

The human will, that force unseen,
The offspring of a deathless soul,
Can hew the way to any goal,
Though walls of granite intervene.

—Ella Wheeler Wilcox

IF a fairy godmother told you she would increase whichever of your powers you named, you would probably say, "Give me more will power."

Most of us feel that we know what we ought to do but think we lack the will power to do it.

This is a mistake. Every person who is not feeble-minded has all the will power he needs to accomplish what he really desires to do. What he lacks is the habit of **exercising** his will power.

Human Electricity

Will power is human electricity. You have enough of this electricity generated in you to achieve the greatest things in life if you will **keep the current on.**

The trouble with us all is that we fail to watch the current. We press the button occasionally and have moments of exultation when we feel that nothing is impossible.

But we allow our minds to relax. The transcendent moment passes and we relapse into the dull feelings of the commonplace.

In this lesson we are going to show you how to keep the current on *all the time* and how to increase it, when necessary, to the highest voltage.

If you will follow these instructions you can do what you want to do, you can have what you want to have. You can make the transcendent moments permanent. You can become a leader, a dominant figure in the place in which you live. ***You can remake your life.***

Not In One Day

Let us make clear at the outset that we do not promise you can do this in a day.

We do not say you can have these rewards for nothing. You must pay a price for them. You must pay a big price.

But what you will get for that price will be worth to you a thousand times more than it costs.

Anything worth having *costs.* Nothing but the undesirable comes free.

We will give you the rules; it is up to you to do the rest. Follow them with even fifty percent of faithfulness and a year from today you will be a changed individual. You will have advanced several rungs in the ladder of success. There will be a conquering gleam in your eyes, more money in your purse, more respect in your soul, and your progress will be noted by all who know you.

If you will give even half your application to these laws, ten years from now you will have made a name for yourself.

The Man of Will

We all want to be able to apply our will power. The man of strong will is more truly a man than all others. The woman of strong will is a superwoman. They are the rulers of the forces in their own world. They do what they set out to do. They know they have power.

They use it to accomplish their aims. They are loved and admired above all others. When you come into contact with them you can fairly feel the force emanating from them ❧❧

Before giving you the laws for building will power, let us tell you some interesting things about will power.

Two Classes of Wills

All the people in the world can be put into two classes with regard to will: those whose wills are overdeveloped, the *impulsive, dare-devil* people with an *over-supply* of will power—and those of *under-developed* wills.

The former have wills so strong they run away with them. The latter have weak wills.

The wills of the former are too energetic. The latter are known as the "lazy willed."

To be successful you must generate your will power to the point where you have as much as those of the over-active will, but *control it* instead of letting *it* control you. You must learn to drive it instead of being driven by it.

In these two classes are eight different kinds of wills. Read this carefully and decide at the outset which are yours.

Inactive Wills

Some people glide along through life without taking any real part in it. They do not seem able to stimulate themselves or to be stimulated. We have in mind the people who let others decide things for them, who have no fixed purpose and who seem incapable of making decisions.

As decision is the first step in will making, these people seem never to have will power.

The Evaders

Have you ever noticed that some people evade every critical situation, refuse to accept responsibility? Their aims seem to point in no direction; they refuse to take a stand even with regard to their own affairs.

Have you noticed how this kind of person evades, how he sidesteps, how he seems to have no definite ideas or attitudes about things?

Have you noticed the kind of person who lets his parents, wife, children or friends decide for him, or who waits for circumstances to decide? This is the *inactive-willed* individual.

Don't Wait on Chance

We know of one such young woman who is being pushed here and there like a chessman on the board, first by this person, then by that, because she refuses to **assume responsibility.**

Like all people who wait for the trend of circumstances instead of "trending circumstances" themselves, she never gets anything she wants.

He who relies on "circumstances" to bring him what he desires will get from those circumstances only the things he does not desire.

Very few desirable things happen to the man who waits on chance.

To get anything worth having you must go after it, keep after it and *hunt it down.*

The crumbs of life are all that fall to him who sits under the table instead of taking his place at the head of the table.

The Indecisive Child

If you have a child who is inclined to let you make his decisions for him, start today to compel him to decide some things *for himself.*

We recently heard a mother say with pride: "I am glad Harold is so obedient. He never decides anything. He leaves it all to me. He does just as I think best in everything. He is a great comfort to me. He is so unlike Mrs. Gregory's boy who can't be dissuaded from what he wants to do." Doubtless Mrs. Gregory envies Harold's mother peace and comfort her amenable son affords her.

But fifteen years from now, if these two boys follow the paths on which they have started, this mother will be envying Mrs. Gregory.

Unquestioned obedience and lack of definite opinions are attractive in babies, *but in no one else*

Life is ruthless. It rides over and grinds into dust every person who cannot stand up for himself.

Doubtless Mrs. Gregory's boy is the bane of her existence today, but he has ten chances to Harold's one when he leaves her side for the world.

It takes definiteness—knowing what you want and when you want it—to win a place for one's self in this world.

The boy who passively submits every question to his parents is a source of comfort as a baby, but a source of humiliation as a man, while the parents of the headstrong child usually live to see the world bow to him as he made *them* bow.

The Incorrigibles

It is interesting to note that the big men and women of this world were all more or less incorrigible as children. The submissive youngsters in their classes who used to get high marks in "deportment" are not heard of.

If you find it easier to let anything or anybody make your decisions for you; if you are always asking to be told what to do about this or that; if you dislike to assume the burden of a decision, you belong in the inactive-willed class.

This tendency, if unchecked, will bring you the remnants, the leavings, and the tail-ends of life. To overcome it, force yourself to see how colorless and uninteresting an individual you are getting to be.

Make Your Own "Advice"

Start with the little things, such as deciding for yourself today where you will eat lunch, instead of waiting for your companions' advice. Gradually work up to the big things in your life.

We do not mean that you should refuse to listen to the advice of others, but we do mean that after hearing that advice you must decide as to *its merits* &

Beware of the weakness of always *seeking advice.*

Remember you must live your own life.

Remember also that no one can see your life as you can see it if you will look.

After you are twenty years of age, if you keep your eyes and ears open, and your mind working, you are a better judge of the little things than anyone else &

After you are thirty if you let others make your big decisions you are sliding down the toboggan to oblivion; you are going to be a *nonentity.*

The Middle-Aged Child

Most of those who are living at home after thirty are really there as a result of their inactive wills.

We know ourselves very little. Our real motives, desires and tendencies lie submerged in the depths of our subconscious.

The woman who at thirty-five is still living at home usually believes in all sincerity what she tells you, that "she has never been able to get away because father and mother needed her."

The truth of it usually is that *she needed father and mother.*

Nine out of ten such women belong in the class of the inactive willed. They cling to home and parents out of the subconscious fear of making decisions, facing responsibility or plunging into the maelstrom of life.

They go to their graves without recognizing this fact. They make a virtue of their vice.

The world calls them "self-sacrificing," forgetting, as Mark Twain said in his essay, "What is Man?" that "Every act of every human being is for the purpose of *contenting his own spirit.*"

Leaning on Parents

If you are over thirty-five and find it easy to wander back home frequently to spend a year or two, you are in danger. Your subconscious is secretly looking for *something to lean on.* Come home occasionally to visit, take care of your parents if necessary, by all means, but don't let them take care of *you.*

You will never develop a great will leaning on your father and mother.

Of course we are not speaking of those whose fathers and mothers live with them, who blaze the trail and face the world to shield their parents.

We are speaking of those who frequently take up their position behind father's and mother's front trench ❧❧

Impulsive Wills

The second are those of the impulsive wills, who seem to "do things without thinking," who have sudden attractions and repulsions, who obey all of these attractions and repulsions, darting down this road and that without making headway *on the main highway* of their lives.

We mean those who decide everything instantly on impulse and who, for this reason, are always being compelled to rescind their decisions and make new ones. We mean those who throw prudence to the winds.

If you are one of these, promise yourself you will not make an instantaneous decision next time but will compel yourself to *think it over.*

Even if you are sure you will ultimately make that decision, hold it in abeyance for a few minutes or hours

In this way you will train yourself to more sober judgments

Overactive Wills

The third is the class called the over-active-willed. These are like the impulsive-willed but more diffuse

They make decisions on everything and begin the action on those decisions.

They are the people whom we think of as having a "whirlwind of plans" all the time, who have many irons in the fire, who lay out too many kinds of activities for themselves.

The remedy for these is to realize that life is short, that the man who attempts too much gets nowhere. They should focus. If you belong to this class and will specialize, you will accomplish great things, for this is one of the most powerful wills and one of the most desirable when properly directed.

Discouraged Wills

The fourth is the "discouraged will"—the will of the individual who has tried *so many times and failed* that he says now, "I can't. I have no will power. It is no use. I have tried so often and failed so completely there is no use."

These people see and know what they should do but refuse to try again. They are superior to those of the inactive wills, for they have made efforts. They deserve credit for their attempts.

If you belong to this class, read the instructions in this lesson, adhere to them, and you can do *what you* want to do.

Emotional Wills

In the fifth subdivision are those known as "the emotional willed." They are characterized by their intense feelings. These are the people who *feel* more than they *think.* They decide everything on their feelings and moods.

Usually the mood or the emotion is so intense that they let it go at that.

It is a well-known psychological fact that we act only to *rid ourselves of pent up tensions.*

When the emotional-willed finds a temporary outlet for his feelings, he is inclined not to act on his decision. He is going down the street, sees a man injured, decides with tears in his eyes to do something to help him, gets the man's name and determines to call at the hospital next day to find out what he can do for the family.

But before the next day arrives he has so completely vented his emotion in telling the story to his friends, he never goes to the hospital!

If you have an emotional will, don't make rash promises on your feelings, for feelings have a way of oozing out. Look yourself in the eye and realize that too much emotional tensity will prevent your putting anything through.

The next time you find yourself *deeply sympathetic, furiously angry or exultantly happy*, don't let that emotional self in temporary control trick you into deciding things.

It is always better to avoid making the decision you are not likely to carry out, because the failure to live up to it has a tendency to rob you of your self-respect 🙷🙷

Vacillating Wills

The sixth class is closely allied with the emotionals and is called the "vacillating-willed." These people change their minds so often before action takes place that they accomplish very little. They waste their energy making decisions which they never carry out.

The man who says, "I will see Jones today and make those arrangements," and who ten minutes later says, "No, I won't do that, I'll wait and see Brown," usually lets the day go by without seeing either.

We know a young man who has this kind of will. He plans on giving Thursday evening to attending a serious lecture on a subject in which he is interested.

But when Thursday evening comes he says, "I don't feel in the mood for that tonight. I want to do something else. I want to be cheered up. I want a thrill. I am going to see some vaudeville." Before the performance is half over he leaves, regretting that the lecture is also over.

If you classify yourself with the "vacillating- willed," put the brakes on when you find yourself making decisions wholesale.

Train yourself to look the ground over every morning; to decide what is best to do. Then don't allow yourself to make **too many** changes.

Practical Wills

The seventh are the "practical-willed."

These people see everything from the **practical** standpoint. They are the other extreme from the emotional and vacillating, but in the end get more out of life.

These are the people who live in the **ruts** and **grinds** of daily details and routine, who never have one grand overpowering purpose.

They are the ones who must do a certain thing on Monday, another on Tuesday, another on Thursday, another on Sunday, because they decided, perhaps years ago, that it was advisable to do these things on these days.

They pride themselves on their "will power," forgetting that the will should be a servant to reason, and if the reason has changed the will current should be turned to *fit the new conditions.*

These people are inclined to be narrow. They are the human penny-in-the-slot machines.

If you find yourself adhering to the schedules of five years ago without making improvements in them; if you cannot adapt yourself to the exigencies of new situations; if you refuse to bend to the plans of others occasionally, you do have will power ❧❧

But you are paying more for it than it is worth. Its current will not carry you far unless you learn to direct it according to the *needs and merits* of each situation instead of to *preconceived* conditions.

Purposive Wills

The eighth and last subdivision is the one in which we all hope to be classed and in which to a great extent you may put yourself if you will follow the rules of this lesson.

These are the "purposive-willed "—those who decide what they want to do after looking over the merits of the case, who *gather their forces and get there* ❧❧

In this class are those who make up their minds as you make up a train, turn on the steam and go ahead to their destination. It is this kind of will which has marked all great men and women.

Will That Won Woman Suffrage

This will is strikingly exemplified by that great leader of the Woman Suffrage Movement, Carrie Chapman Catt.

That her purposive will has been to a great extent responsible for the emancipation of American women is a fact too well known to need an echo from us.

But the following sidelight on will power in general is too significant to leave untold.

A few years ago we had occasion to spend a few days in the little Iowa town whose chief pride is that this international figure spent her girlhood there.

Inasmuch as a leading American magazine had, the month previous, printed a symposium of the opinions of prominent Europeans and Americans to the effect that Carrie Chapman Catt was considered the leading woman of the English speaking races, we were much interested in the psychology of her girlhood friends.

One evening at a gathering of these we asked them in what way, if any, she seemed different from them when they were all children together.

"Nothing," they said, "Carrie was just like the rest of us as far as we could see, except this: whenever she made up her mind to do anything she always did it. *She put through whatever she started.*"
❧❧

Brain-Training

"How is it possible to build will power?" you ask. The answer is simple. It is also scientific. Your brain is living protoplasm and *living protoplasm can be trained.*

If we told you we could teach you how to develop your body muscles to the point of physical efficiency you would not question it.

In this lesson we are going to show you how to train your brain muscles. This is simpler than training your bodily muscles, because your brain has much greater susceptibility, is capable of far greater change and development.

Will is *directed desire.* It is not a mere matter of thinking. It is *thinking* plus *feeling.* Thoughts are cold, but feelings are warm, alive, vital.

Learn How To Want

The first law in building will power is: ***Learn to desire.*** You must not only wish—you must ***want.*** You must stir your nature to its very depths if you would gain anything great.

Desire — passion — emotion — wanting — demanding — these are the things that create.

Do not stop thinking, wishing, yearning or longing for the things you want.

If your ambition is worthwhile, let it ***possess you***, give it a free rein. If it isn't worthy, ***get one*** that is

To create a thing you must ***want*** it with a burning want that recognizes no refusal—that brooks no denial.

Wanters and Wishers

Every leader of men is characterized by the ***intensity*** of his desires. You never hear him say he "wishes" he could do a thing. He says, "I ***want*** to do it."

That wanting, that burning determination kindles desires in those around him, makes them want to help him get it, makes them follow him, and these in turn incite him to further action.

Whenever you come in contact with a man of intense desire you feel the force radiating from him. You feel he has learned how to concentrate that force on things he wanted to do.

No Non-Essentials

Let us give you here the second law for building will power: ***Eliminate the non-essentials.***

The big man focuses his strength on the important things, the ***vital things.*** He doesn't even see the superficial, unnecessary, trivial things that would sap his energy.

Just as Attention is the secret of Worry and Visualization the secret of Self-Confidence, **Concentration** is the big basic secret of Will Power.

Any man who will keep his mind concentrated on what he wants will get it.

This is due to the psychological law that ***our actions follow our thoughts.***

You express will power a hundred times a day. If you think you lack it tell me what it is that enables you to get up in the morning; what it is that has made possible everything you have ever achieved.

We will take a familiar example. You desire to move your foot—and it moves. Why? Because this wonderful mysterious force stored up within you is the electrical current you have released to move your foot. This current can only be generated by ***desire*** ❦❦

Don't Be A Pigeon

Most people in the world do not know ***how*** to desire. They do not know what it is to be filled with an eager, intense craving, longing, ravenous desire that takes possession of them and makes them ***demand*** things of life instead of asking for them ❦❦

They are like sheep, rabbits or pigeons who sit meekly around while the strong ones of the race—those filled with these burning desires—gather up every good thing in sight!

There is in this, as in all natural laws, a kind of justice. Those who do not exercise the force which nature has given them cannot people the world with strong souls.

Open the Door

Any man with will power can open the door to what he wants. More of us sit on the doorstep crying for it to open.

Will power is more than a mere faculty of the mind. It is a mighty attribute. Buxton said, "I am more certain the longer I live that the greatest difference between men, between the weak and the strong, the great and the small, is energy-invincible determination—*a* purpose once fixed, and then ***victory or death.***

"Will power will do anything that can be done in this world. No talents, no conditions, no opportunities, will make a two-legged man without it."

Have a Purpose

Disraeli said, "I have brought myself, after long meditation, to the conviction that a human being with a settled purpose can accomplish it, that ***nothing*** can resist a will which will stake existence, if need be, on its fulfillment."

The secret of resolute will is found in persistence and determination. Learn **tenacity of attention**—concentration.

You must learn to concentrate your will upon a thing and not allow it to be distracted or wander off until you have ***done*** what you have set out to do. This can be done by following the triple methods set forth in this lesson.

First, stir up your desire—make it ***live***; second, determine that ***you will*** do it, and third, ***act.*** Millions of men have done these things and so may you.

Will and Habit

At first your greatest enemy will be habit. But habit is a thing that can be changed. Your habits are now enemy habits.

If you will follow the rules of this lesson your habits will be your friends.

The thing you call your weak will is not a weak will but a load of ***detrimental habits.*** You created these habits. You can demolish them. You created them by giving them your vote when you might have voted for something better.

Every person is an Ego with two individualities—a weak self and a strong self.

The weak self always takes the easy way out; it is lazy, inert, made up of our lower urges.

The stronger self may be said to be composed of our higher urges, such as aspiration and altruism.

If you are enslaved to bad habits it is because the ego of you has **cast its vote with the weaker** self so often your giving in to it has become more or less automatic.

To develop your will do not attempt to remake yourself in a day.

"How shall I a habit break?"
"As you did that habit make;
As you gathered, you must lose;
As you yielded, now refuse.
Thread by thread the strands we twist,
Till they bind us, neck and wrist;
Thread by thread, the patient hand
Must untwine till free we stand.
As we builded stone by stone,
We must toil unhelped, alone,
Till the wall is overthrown."

— John Boyle O'Reilly

Just as habit has been allowed to work against you it can now be made to work for you.

Gather the strength to do today a few little things that are not easy and tomorrow they will be easier

Good Habits by Substitution

William James said, "Do not try to destroy your bad habits by force. Make some good ones and *they* will destroy the others."

To do this, first get control of the ***physical channels*** of expression—the channels through which are expressed the mental states of self-confidence

Get control of the muscles through which will power is expressed.

Control your shoulders. Begin to put them back manfully instead of letting them sag.

Get control of the muscles that hold your head up

Control your eyes. Gaze into the face of the world fearlessly

Get control of the muscles of your legs and walk firmly as a positive man does.

Get control of the vocal organs and begin to speak in the vibrant tones which ***command attention and respect.***

We do not know just how it happens but we do know that these things clear a ***channel*** through which will power expresses itself.

Shut Out the Fringes

Learn to keep your mind on ***what you want to do.*** When you have once focused your will on a thing ***hold it there.*** When it runs away, ***bring it back.*** Shut out the fringes.

The Orientals have a word to express the concentration which gets things— "one-pointed."

Put out of your mind all thoughts and ideas that are out of harmony with the big ideal of your life

At first you will have to fight against all manner of distracting thoughts, but after a while you will acquire the habit of turning them away without conscious interruption.

The best method for warding off undesirable thoughts is to keep the mind filled with mental pictures or visualizations of yourself *as doing the thing you wish to do.* This adds oil to the flame of your desire.

Concentration and Will

The art of concentration has up to this time been shrouded in occultism and mystery.

This is due to the fact that its advocates had only empirical knowledge on the subject. They have observed what could be accomplished by concentrative methods, but have had no comprehension of the *reason* for the results achieved.

Absolute concentration means merely the massing of all your thoughts upon a *single purpose.* It means *mental efficiency.* It means drawing your mental fires to *one point* instead of *shooting sparks* into space.

Ordinarily your desires and emotions scatter your energies and exhaust you to no purpose whatever. Organize these powers and the only question then to be answered is, "What shall I go after?"

Mental co-ordination, harmony and unity, such as will lift you out of all petty annoyances, can be yours. Your stream of consciousness is a *living current.* It is a swirling torrent of activity. But its powers have always been under-estimated.

Hold These Two Ideas

Lillian Hartman Johnson, Ph. D., eminent Mental Analyst and authority on the subconscious, says, "Your mental attitude must be made up of but two ideas: 'I am certain to succeed,' and, 'how.' If you will constantly maintain this attitude you will draw from the profoundest depths of your nature the plans and power for doing it."

The Steps Toward Will

We will now give you the specific steps by which you may build your will power and do anything really wish to do ❧❧

No. 1. Awaken the power of willing by realizing that you can *will* to do a thing. In other words, come to a realization of the power and possibilities of the human will, and that you possess one ❧❧

Most people fail to develop will power because they *refuse to will* to do a thing.

At these moments open your mind and let the consciousness of your own ability begin to assert itself. Realize that you are the master of conditions; that you are a dynamo that is continually generating sufficient will power to do great things; recognize that you are in possession, —not your habits, not your weaker self, but the ego—the "I," the soul of you.

One moment after doing this you will lift your chest, you will become conscious—for some inexplicable reason—of resources in which you have hitherto had little confidence.

No. 2. Decide what you want to do.

"Look before you leap" is an old but sensible admonition. Always take a good look before plunging in ❧❧

Exercise your judgment and do not be swayed too much by the judgment of others.

Learn to put your hand to the plow and not turn back ❧❧

Learn to control your will power so that it will not leap into action until you are ready for it to do so.

When you have done this—when you are sure this is the thing you *want* to do—clinch your mind shut and *lock it.*

Make up your mind that your *mind is made is up.* Leave no reservations. Don't say, "This is what I want to do but perhaps tomorrow I shall feel differently." ❧❧

Don't decide until you are as sure as it is humanly possible to be, and then *stick.*

No. 3. Gather together in your mind all the **advantages** you will gain from doing this thing.

Visualize yourself as doing it. See yourself enjoying the comforts, spending the money it would bring, meeting the friends, the pleasurable situations, accepting the honors, reaping all the rewards that would follow.

Say that the thing upon which you have bent your will is a college education. Keep yourself reminded of the many advantages of a college education. Picture to yourself the friendships you would make, the learning you would acquire, the **person you would become** with this new development ✷✷

See yourself in college. Picture yourself as going through that four years, from your freshman year to your cap-and-gown-days.

Let your mind dwell on the joys of intellectual growth, the fun you will have in athletic sports, general college activities—everything from spreads to "exams."

Remind yourself that the experiences of those four years will change your life, will open the doors of opportunity and romance.

Picture to yourself the upstanding, clear-eyed, capable young person you are going to be at the end of those four years, equipped with learning to meet the world.

No. 4. Gather together in your mind all the **penalties** and **punishments** that would come from not doing this thing you wish to do. Dwell on them. Paint them in their darkest colors.

Picture to yourself the embarrassments and humiliations which will accrue as a result of not going to college. Think of the opportunities for promotion, advancement—financial and otherwise —which you will be cheated out of if you do not get a college education.

Recall how much less self-confidence the man without a college education feels; think how this handicap will affect your life.

No. 5. Announce your plans to those who are truly interested in you. We want you to do this because it gives your pride a powerful *incentive;* having once declared you are going to college, you have something to *live up to.*

One of the most conspicuous tricks of your weaker self is to get you *not to let your friends know* of your good resolutions.

You give yourself all manner of reasons for keeping still, but the *real* one is that this miserable little weaker side of your nature has whispered to you, "Don't tell anybody, then if you fail it will be no disgrace."

This gives you every chance to lose. It means leaving the back door unlocked, ready for your desertion if you become too cowardly to go out the front.

We do not mean by this that you should go about publishing your plans to everybody. Never tell them to any but those who are in sympathy with you, who like you and are *interested in you.*

You will then not only be impelled to do what you have set out to do in order to keep their respect, but will be *inspired* by their belief in you and their desire to see you win.

No. 6. Weld the *thought of doing* to the *action of doing* by the only thing that ever welds anything—*feeling* ઠઠ

Watch the blacksmith when he is trying to weld together two pieces of iron. He builds a fire under them. Mere thoughts are cold things, but feelings are alive!

Let yourself feel intensely about this thing you want to do. The white heat of emotion will compel you to act. Feeling arouses the will, and the *will stimulates action.* These two act and react upon each other. They work in unison. The trained individual has both under control, *pulling together* like a well trained team.

No. 7. Avoid all friends, situations and conditions that would *interfere* with what you wish to do.

If you have been associating with superficial people who care for nothing but dances, movies, parties and fun, and who are out of sympathy with the idea of a college education, begin to give them *less of your time.* Understand them, give them tolerance; never feel bigoted or superior. But learn how to **stay away from them.**

Refuse to make engagements with people whose ideals, standards and convictions pull you away from your aims.

Remember the legend of Ulysses, who induced his companions to stop up their ears with wax lest they be fascinated by the songs of the sirens.

It is much easier to listen to the songs of the sirens of idleness, ease, pleasure and dissipation. But eventually it takes you down.

No. 8. Put yourself in the way of friends, situations and conditions **conducive to your aim.**

This is not difficult. If you are truly interested in a college education you will attend the lectures, visit the libraries, and frequent the other places where college people, and those who hope to be college people, **are to be found.** You will soon make new friends, friends who will aid you, encourage you, inspire you.

If it is necessary that you leave the town in which you live in order to find congenial companions, do so. Go **anywhere**, at any cost, to surround yourself with the things which will **help** and not hinder.

No. 9. Start today. Take at least one step toward your goal.

Don't try to take too long a step. Start at the easiest end of this thing you wish to do. Do not attempt the hardest part at first, only be sure that you do something **right now.**

Do not attempt to start to college today, but do not let the sun go down without at least writing a letter, looking up a catalogue or doing **something** toward a real start.

Do not let the size of your task discourage you. The greatest struggle is always at the beginning ☦☦

Start slowly. Gird on your armor, grasp your sword, but don't attempt to finish the whole fight in one day.

Plan to increase the tasks each day. Plan to do something bigger and bigger each week. Do not be like the man who wanted to jump a ditch but never did because whenever he got to it he ran back for a fresh start.

No. 10. Do this thing *one day at a time.*

Most of those who fail to develop will power have been frightened out by the feeling of the *"unendingness"* of the task. Under the weight of all the future, they succumbed before they started ❧❧

Don't let the thought of the "foreverness" enter your mind. Stand up to it a minute, an hour at a time.

Professor James said, "The man who attempts to do only today's work today can accomplish wonders." ❧❧

It is the convulsive worker who breaks down.

It is the man who lets the thought of *the tomorrows* get into his mind who cannot live up to today.

Never be in a hurry; do not let anxiety and solicitude for results terrorize you. Work systematically—economize effort. *Waste no time regretting the past or fearing the future.*

No. 11. Do not let exceptions occur.

Beware of your weaker self when it whispers, "You have proven you can do this, now take a little vacation." ❧❧

The actual interruption would not always do you harm. It is the *memory* of the exception which poisons. This makes you lose faith in yourself.

Having once allowed a break in the chain, you feel less equal to building a strong one. You are ashamed; you are conscience-stricken; you are fully aware, *after it is done,* that it was your weaker self that induced you to do it. This realization is disintegrating.

Remember then that one interruption can undo the good work of weeks. It is like a ball of twine. The carelessness of an instant can unwind it.

No. 12. As a reminder of your will power, let every good thought for the first few days express itself in *some kind of action.*

At the same time, see how many unpleasant or unkind thoughts you can inhibit. Every good thought which evaporates without action leaves you weaker, while the conquering of an unkind thought gives you strength.

No. 13. Every day do something you **do not like to do.** Everyone, even the weakest, can do things they like to do—pleasant, agreeable things. But these are not the proof of real will power.

Nothing will encourage you more, nothing will prove to you your own powers like compelling yourself to do something disagreeable.

Professor James advised his students systematically to exercise themselves in the direction of doing some particular things for no other reason than that they **preferred not** to do them, even if the task be nothing more than giving up one's seat in a street car. He said: "Doing daily a disagreeable thing is like paying the premiums of insurance on one's property. It is laying up reserve resources for the day of need."

But it is even more necessary that you keep up your will insurance. Your property may never burn down, but the emergencies in your own life which call for will power are inevitable. Only the man who has trained himself to do the hard thing can meet these emergencies when they arrive.

James said: "The men who have attained great success have in nearly every case so trained their wills by doing things whether they liked them or not that they could undertake difficult or disagreeable tasks with a minimum of effort. They have acquired the habit."

No. 14. When you do fail, see to it that your will **never condones nor consents.** Let disgust for yourself fill you. But not discouragement. There is a world of difference between disgust and discouragement. There is no reason for discouragement. Nothing was ever done in a day.

No. 15. When successful, tell yourself and your friends of the little victories you have achieved. Do not be conceited about it. Merely tack up a little bulletin in your own mind.

This will give you new pride in yourself. It will give your friends new faith in you, and *their* faith in you will act as a constant urge to you.

No. 16. Avoid all stimulants. They slip the belt off your will. We know a woman who says she does not dare trust herself to go shopping after she has had black coffee. "I spend money like a drunken sailor," she says. Many students have told us how various stimulants affect them, and it is always for the worse.

No. 17. Keep before your mind the ***memory of the feelings*** you have experienced the last time you failed.

Many a man has kept himself at his helm, not because he could not face the prospect of his failure, but because he could not bear it ***in retrospect.***

No. 18. Keep before your mind the memories of how you *felt* ***when you won.*** Live again those feelings of exultation, glory and triumph, than which life holds no greater joy.

No. 19. Keep your mind centered on the thing you wish to do. No matter how great a break may have occurred, bring it back and put it to work again. Eventually it will know better than to wander away

No. 20. Set aside the last ten minutes of each day to revisualize your desire, to live over again your reasons for making your decision.

One of the best aids to will power is to make a list, during this ten minutes, of the things to do next day

Look over this list each evening and scratch off those you have done. Transfer those undone to the next day's sheet. If you have an ounce of pride you cannot bear to leave many of these undone tasks to stare you in the face at night.

No. 21. Never mistake ***stubbornness*** for strength. Stubbornness is the result of prejudice, ignorance or misdirected energy. The stubborn man cannot yield. The strong man knows that yielding is sometimes the greatest proof of strength.

The Grand Canyon was made by trickling drops of water that changed their courses many times but the goal never.

Sometimes it is necessary to turn slightly aside in order to achieve one's ultimate goal, just as the little drops of water had to turn aside and wind their way around the pebbles, rocks and boulders in the construction of that sublimest masterpiece.

The man with the strong will knows how to yield. He knows that yielding sometimes means stepping aside to get a better view or a stronger foothold

The stubborn man will not bend nor stoop and often this stiff attitude breaks him.

A willow bends when a storm is on, but bobs up and keeps growing after it has passed. A ship turns out of its course to avoid rocks and icebergs.

The big man does not push ahead into the very face of trouble just because his original path pointed that way. He weaves, winds, stoops, climbs over, goes around, under, and gets there!

No. 22. Make every act one of *vigor.*

Do not do anything half-heartedly.

Do not hold back.

Play fair with yourself. Merely going through the *motions* of what you have decided to do is cheating yourself

When you have decided to do a thing, not only do it but do it *well*, do it *hard*, do it *to a finish.* In no other way can the maximum of strength be acquired

No. 23. Keep the realization that you are winning. See yourself as the man who is conquering himself. *Never admit defeat.*

No. 24. Do not relax in your efforts. When you get to the places where you feel incapable of making further headway just then, do not give up. At least *hold your own.*

Be like the swimmer who, when he reaches an adverse tide, manages to hold himself up even though he may make no progress.

No. 25. Note with what ***surprising ease*** you do these things which you considered were going to be hard.

Keep yourself reminded of the psychological fact that it is never the DOING of a thing that makes it difficult; it is our ANTICIPATION of it. In this way you will acquire a consciousness of your own self-mastery.

If you will follow these rules you can train the vast forces of your mind to act in accordance with your will. You can build will power. Thus, and thus only, have all things worth while been done in this world.

LESSON VII

___

How to Make Money

"If I just had a chance! There are chances aplenty
Right close to our fingertips, day after day,
For each opportunity seized there are twenty
Overlooked and permitted to wander away.

And while we are waiting for someone to offer
Ways for winning success by some 'push-button' plan,
With the splendid rewards she is eager to proffer,
Opportunity sighs: 'If I just had a man!'"

—Edgar A. Guest

THE subject of money-making is an interesting one for many reasons. It is the one upon which more thoughts are centered, about which more lies are told, and concerning which more deception is practiced than any other in the world. All of us want to make money—but few admit it.

"The Double Standard" of Money

This is due to the false training we receive. From early childhood we are taught that to want money is an ignominious ambition; that it is something to be ashamed of.

Very young or very gullible people believe in the sincerity of those who preach this doctrine.

But at along about eleven years they begin to wake up. They discover gradually that the "double standard of morals" is nothing to the **double standard of money!**

They begin to discover that underneath all this piety there runs a burning desire for the 'root of all evil." They discover later that those who prate oftenest, loudest and longest against money-making have an eagle-eye focused on getting all they can of it for themselves.

The Pious "Pillar"

A lecturer, speaking on this subject, said recently: "I was about nine when a realization of this came to me.

"One Sunday I was passing the collection basket in church, as a substitute for one of the ushers who was not there that day.

"In my section there was one of the well-to-do pillars.' I thought he would drop in a big donation for I had heard him make such feeling talks on 'the higher good,' and the sin of 'seeking the things of this world.' So I was looking most intently for it when I passed him the basket.

"From that day to this I have refused to lean too heavily on 'pillars.' He put in a pewter slug!" ❧❧

Plain Talk, Not Platitudes

If you have read this book carefully up to this point (which you have not, for you are reading this lesson **first!**), you have noticed we do not deal in platitudes. We have not once said,

"Genius is an infinite capacity for taking pains," or that "Virtue is its own reward."

Having sidestepped these popular pitfalls we are going to see if we can't be sincere with you to the end. The speaker continued:

"I want to make money. I want to make lots of money and more money every year. And I believe I will, for my income is constantly increasing, due largely to the fact that all who have dealings with me advise their friends to come to me.

"When I ask them why they give me so much free advertising, they say, 'Because you are honest with us. This makes us trust you at the start. At the finish we tell our friends about your lecture courses and publications because we have gotten so much more than our money's worth.'

"I relate this here for two reasons. First, because I believe in advertising, and second, because my experience has proved to me that it is not necessary to deceive people in order to make money 🙖🙖

"Therefore, the first rule for money making is—***don't lie about it.***"

Be Frank About Money

Other people are just as smart as you are.

Don't be an ostrich. Don't stick your head into the sand, imagining no one can see you.

The poets and singers praise the beauties of poverty, the joys of the simple life and tell us about the emptiness of riches.

But even as they say it, they are wondering where they are going to get next month's rent and longing for the riches they condemn.

The "Glamour" of Poverty

There is no glamour over poverty except to the man who has ***climbed out of it.*** There is no halo around hardship except to him who has ***emancipated himself from it.***

When you hear rich Mr. So and so declare he'd "love to go back and live over again the early days when he was poor," do not doubt him.

He thinks he means it. He thinks how he would enjoy the struggle, ***with today's riches in mind.*** He feels that with the certain knowledge that today's riches were on the way he could stand anything ❧❧

One can stand **almost anything** if he knows it is only **temporary.** Poverty and struggle have a halo around them only when you **know they won't last,** only when you know the reward is inevitable. Then the thought of the reward sustains ❧❧

The millionaire would not for anything return to the days when he had to save pennies unless the fairy godmother will allow him to take along the **certainty of today's wealth.**

Don't Be Ashamed About Money

If you want to make money, don't apologize for it ❧❧

Sarah H. Young, well-known efficiency expert, says: "Wanting what money brings is a laudable ambition. Nobody wants money **for its own sake.** Dollars, as dollars, are as valueless as so many pieces of iron.

"We want what money represents—the **comforts** it will provide, the **freedom** it assures, the **self-expression** it guarantees.

The desire for these things is what distinguishes modern men and women from cave dwellers ❧❧

"Without the urge for these things—esthetic surroundings, self-expression and individual freedom—civilization would be unknown. We would still be living in caves, eating raw meat from the bones of wild beasts.

"There would be no art, no literature, no education, no invention, no human liberty, no ideals.

"These are the hungers and cravings that have urged man up from the sod; that have impelled him to face hardships, danger and death,—and thus grow."

Developing Under Pressure

No organism develops except under pressure. We are so full of laziness and inertness that there would have been no development had it not been for this pressure from within. There would be no such thing as evolution ❧❧

The stage to which any creature has evolved can be pretty accurately measured by his ***ambitions and aspirations*** ❧❧

The man who is content to live in poverty, dirt and sordidness —the man who is willing to work all his life at ***some other man's game***—does not greatly advance civilization.

The Lure of Laziness

The man who turns his back on the lure of laziness and faces the battle with the world, as every man does who makes money, proves thereby that he has ambition and energy.

To such men and women we owe the cultivation of the fields, the clearing of the forests, the building of cities, the invention of the steam engine, the telegraph, telephone, wireless, aviation, all the vehicles of human progress.

Because a few safe-blowers, capitalists, etc., have used their brains to get money unethically, does not alter these facts.

Abuse Proves Nothing

Every great thing is carried to the point of abuse by some. Money making on the stupendous scale practiced by a few multi-millionaires no more discredits the normal money making instinct than the over-eating of a few gluttons discredits the instinct of eating.

All extremes are dangerous to the individual and to the race.

For both these reasons money-making as it is practiced today by combines, to the enslavement of the workers and the fleecing of the consumer, ***must be*** and ***will be abolished.***

Our Right to the Best

This lesson is no brief for the man who gets money dishonestly, be he porch-climber or magnate. It is for all who desire the best life can give us, who believe we are entitled to the best and who are willing to win it in the open by *honorable methods.*

It is for those who realize that *nothing worthwhile comes free.*

It is for those who realize, however, that everything, even money, comes easier than we anticipate, *if we only go after it.*

Hubbard said: "Blessed is he who is not looking for a soft snap for he is the only one who shall find it." ❧❧

It Won't Fall into Your Lap!

If you are looking for a secret whereby you may make money overnight in an easy, leisurely way, you are booked for disappointment.

There are no wonderful secrets about making money. There are certainly no easy, carefree, comfortable roads to the land of Wealth. This is the first thing you must realize.

The rules for making money are simple rules, but they are not easy to follow.

It takes *stamina* to make money.

It takes *backbone* and *jawbone* rather than *wishbone* ❧❧

It takes will power.

The Cat by the Fire

But do not let this depress you. "Will power," as Arnold Bennett said, "is the chief thing that differentiates you from the cat by the fire."

If you prefer the cat-by-the-fire existence to the rich rewards of effort, give up this lesson. Also give up the hope of ever getting *anything worthwhile in this world.*

Above we told you that the first step in making money is to be straightforward *concerning your money making aspirations.* The money-making aspiration is the mark of the man who has evolved beyond the cat-by-the fire stage.

Money Usually Measures Service

The money a man makes may be one of the truest measures of his service to mankind.

The world is full of people who want all kinds of things, who need all kinds of things for material and spiritual advancement.

They stand ready and anxious to pay in real dollars and other rewards the man or woman who will supply those needs.

Whenever you see a penniless man you see a man who is not producing much, if anything, for the satisfaction of these needs, the alleviation of these sufferings, or inspiration for the battles of the people OF TODAY.

The Two Biggest Words

Because they are the most important words we have used up to this time, let us impress upon you the two words in that last sentence.

You may paint the pictures, write the poems, preach the religious and economic doctrine for which future generations will immortalize you, but these achievements will never bring you financial independence unless the world OF TODAY wants them.

"Fame is the food of the tomb." The man who prefers food today to these ashes of immortality must do something, say something, make something or sell something THE PEOPLE OF HIS DAY AND AGE want. They will pay money only for what they want, not for what future generations will want.

Tragic But True

That "Three cities claimed Homer dead through which the living Homer begged his bread," is tragic, but just as true today as it was three thousand years ago.

The roads of yesterday are strewn with the bodies of martyrs whose works vastly benefit us.

We are today martyring other men and women equally good, equally great, whose ideas and productions will vastly advance posterity.

We are starving some of them to death just as our predecessors starved the good and great of their day ☞☞

This Generation Needs

All this is a sad commentary but bemoaning it does not alter human nature.

The man who wishes to make sufficient money to obtain the refinements, self-expression and freedom he craves while he is still alive to enjoy them must produce something *this generation wants* ☞☞

He must not ask that it pay him for a thing its great-great-grand children will want.

Each generation insists on spending its money for the things that meet *its* particular needs, and leaves its descendants to pay their own bills *when they get here.* That the great poet, painter, reformer or teacher will not live that long makes no difference to them.

"Letting Posterity Do It"

"Besides," human nature argues, "how do we know that posterity will want what this man has to offer? Only time can tell whether he is right or wrong. There is no way of distinguishing between the false and the true gods. We will leave it to the future."

The false ones pass; the true have laurels laid on their graves down through the ages.

The "Trend of the Times"

This lesson is for the man and woman who believe that it is as worthy to meet the needs of today's children as those of tomorrow's, and that the benefactors of mankind have a right to the good things which God has filled the world.

Keep your eyes, ears and mind open. Find out what the world wants—the trend of the times what the latest needs are from neckwear to aviation, and see if you can't *devise* something, *improve* something, *invent* something, *organize* something, or *promote* something to *meet these needs.*

Find Your Vocation

To do this, recognize the fact that you were born with talents for doing some of these *much easier than others.*

Find out what these inborn trends are—what you are best fitted for—and then *capitalize them.*

Blaze a Few Trails!

Don't be afraid of an idea because it is your own idea. As Emerson said, "A man discards his thoughts simply because they are his."

All the big money is made by the men who are willing to take at least some risk and blaze trails ◆◆

Don't wait till you see others breaking the trail before you bring forth your vision, for if you do, you get what followers always get—*the leavings.*

The big rewards never go to those who seek the sheltering safety of the second trench, no matter how hard they may actually work *after they start.* Great rewards are never given for work but for *daring.*

The Value of An Idea

Alexander Graham Bell, inventor of the telephone, was asked what he would say were he asked to put into twenty words his best advice to young men who wished to make money. He said: "I would say to young men and young women, 'Get an idea of your own, stick to it, and put all your heart and soul into it every day.' "

Cultivate your initiative. The world reserves its supreme rewards for but one thing—initiative.

Worry and Money-Making

The next big step is to eliminate *worry about money.* Turn back to Lesson I of this course and learn how to do it.

A common sense care for your financial future is necessary, but worry over it only decreases your financial ability.

In these days of keen competition, with everybody else wanting the money you are after, the man who gets it is the one whose mind is given to the work that produces it, not worrying *for fear he won't make it.*

The man whose attention is centered on the fear of poverty, *brings about the very poverty he fears.*

Your actions match your predominant thoughts ❖❖

The man whose thoughts are of poverty *acts like poverty.* Nobody dares to trust a high-salaried job to him.

High salaries are never paid for *manual* work. They are paid to the men who do *mental work*—thinking out *constructive ideas.*

The mind that is all clogged up with poverty worries is not in good running order. What you accomplish is due to the *working out of ideas, and such a mind can't produce ideas.*

From Your Neck Up!

A great financier said once, "From the neck down a man is worth $3 a day. From the neck up a man may be worth anywhere from $10,000 to several hundred thousand dollars a year."

Work Your Head!

Another millionaire is fond of saying, "The difference between the hod carrier and the $50,000-a-year-man is that the hod carrier works his hod and the other man works his head."

The World Is Looking For Them

A friend of J. Pierpont Morgan once said to him, "I need a man with ideas. If you should find such a man and will send him to me I will pay him $50,000 a year." "If I find that man," said Morgan, one who can be eyes and ears for me when I'm not there *you will never lay eyes on him*, for I shall pay him $100,000 a year."

Where Ideas Come From

Right here is a good place to tell you a great psychological law: Ideas come to us as the result of *concentrating on the things we want.*

We don't mean that you must cut yourself of from your friends and family, shut yourself up in a quiet room and fasten your conscious mind on what you want, though a few moments of this daily is most effective.

We mean rather the constant thinking in the *back of your mind* about the thing you want—plus a *striving after it.*

Psychologists have named this chamber in the back of your mind the subconscious. It is your "silent partner." It takes orders from you. It will work on whatever subject you wish. What is more, it will work on that subject *until you tell it to stop.*

Money-Making and The Subconscious

Your subconscious is about 90 per cent of your mind 🙰🙰

When you worry, this great working force is expended in negative, destructive work. All of its strength is used up in this way. There is then none left with which to plan out the things you want.

If you expect to get what you **want,** instead of what you **fear,** change the standing order to your subconscious.

Instead of letting it spend its time loafing in the movie theatre of your mind—in that chamber of horrors where your fears are on parade—order it to come out into the sunshine right now and get busy *figuring out ways and means to get what you want* 🙰🙰

Nothing Fails Like Failure

If you are worried everybody knows it.

Nothing fails like failure.

Stop giving failure thoughts a place in your mental power house.

Study the successful man. You will note that under all circumstances he *radiates success.* He does not always have the material facts and reasons justifying it.

But material things are born of spiritual things, and the man who, in the days of no business, keeps up a successful front ultimately has a *successful business.*

Personal Appearance

In this connection we can mention the matter of personal appearance and its influence on success 🙰🙰

A young man once asked an American millionaire how he should dress to be successful.

"As though you were *already successful,*" he answered. And that is the law of self-confidence and of all success—TO ACT THE PART IF YOU WANT TO MAKE IT REAL.

Its Effect on You

The effect that your dress, your grooming and your general appearance have on *you* is fully as important as its effect on others.

No one has ever yet fully defined the psychology of dress, but it is certain that there is a mysterious relationship between one's personal appearance and his self-respect.

It not only helps or hinders success but helps or hinders character and moral courage.

"Clean linen is," as a great writer once said, "a source of spiritual strength second only to that of a clean conscience."

We know a Milwaukee woman who will not meet any one she wishes to impress without wearing a red rose and immaculate white gloves.

A Good Habit

One of the most successful men of our acquaintance says that whenever he has a big deal to put through, even if it comes in the middle of the day, he goes home, takes a shower bath, shaves and dresses throughout with fresh garments.

"This may sound silly to you," he said. "I laugh at myself for doing it, but I have found it pays."

Even if you are not like this man, and do not see the importance of dress, you must take it into consideration.

The Price You Pay

If you are not naturally particular about yourself; if you are inclined to be a little slack or slovenly; if you are careless one or two mornings a week and hurry off to work without the usual touches to your toilet, *you are paying a high price for it*

You cannot afford this handicap.

Dress makes a tremendous difference in your chances for success. Don't ignore it.

One of the best investments you can make is in putting up a good appearance.

Say what you will about the unimportance of clothes in comparison with the man himself, we all realize that our clothes do cut a big figure in people's estimate of us.

We know that the impression other people get of us has a *far reaching influence* on our lives.

Clothes play a leading part in our general appearance and our general appearance is responsible for the big part of that impression ❧❧

Dress Your Front Window!

Clothes do not make the man, but good clothes have got many a man a good job that he never would have had otherwise. And a man with a good job has a chance to become a better man.

Your personal appearance, your dress, your manner, your grooming, your haircut and hair dress are the front windows which advertise, as all show windows do, the *stock of goods inside.*

The way a merchant displays his goods is the first step in salesmanship. If his windows are filled with soiled, out-of-date wares, if they do not indicate care, system and order, you expect to find the same characteristics inside, and you will.

Each His Own Salesman

You are a salesman. Every person in the world is a salesman of something, whether he is selling commodities or not.

You are anxious to succeed; you wish to get a good position—in other words, sell your services—you want to make the most of yourself that is, market your abilities most effectively and for the highest possible price. You want friendship, love and marriage. Even love and friendship are exchanges, and therefore a kind of salesmanship ❧❧

Where Do People Place You?

Where people place you in their estimation has a powerful effect on your career. They place an estimate upon you, consciously or unconsciously, the instant they lay their eyes on you.

It is never as easy to change that estimate afterward as it would have been to make the *right impression the first time.*

Because your personal appearance is the first thing people see about you it should be worthy of you, of your best and highest self.

We do not mean extravagantly handsome dress; we mean refined, inconspicuous but *tasteful* dress—and *perfect cleanliness.*

Please the Eye First

Because the eye is the favorite sense messenger and the quickest, you must first *please the eye* of the other fellow.

Then you must please his ear.

Later, if you get past these boys in the front office, he may give you a chance to prove your worth, to show him *who* and *what* you are.

Many a superior man, and countless superior women, have failed miserably because they never passed muster with these under-secretaries.

Don't Live For Economy

Many a man has failed because he tried to be *too economical.* He did not keep freshened up with clean linen. He attempted to save on his clothes by having them mended and pressed when he should have gone without food if necessary to buy a new suit.

Wearing shabby clothing and soiled collars has cost hundreds of men their best chances.

Few people realize what a tremendous influence appearances have on their future.

They do not realize when they apply for a position that the mind of their would-be employer is working at lightning-like speed, sizing up whether or not this applicant would be an *asset* or a *liability* to his business.

No matter how many letters of introduction you carry, nor who has written them, they will not get you a good place if your personal appearance is a *poor advertisement of you.*

Meet the Facts

In Philadelphia we saw a sign over the employment manager's window which read, "No seedy looking people wanted here." That this must have been a cruel blow to the poor seedy ones who most needed the *jobs didn't alter the fact.*

And we thought as we looked at it, "The world is like that; it has this over its doorway in letters so big that all who run may read."

We do not say it is right. We say most emphatically it is not right. The standards are wrong.

But they are here.

The Here and Now

Our task in this lesson is not to discuss ethics, but to show you how to achieve happiness and success *here and now,* in this world in which you live. You have the right to both.

As Time is measured, you have but a day to live and the world is not going to be made right in a day ❧❧

If you would be a true success, lift your voice for the ideal world.

Keep working for something better for all humanity but *prove your right to lead humanity* by fulfilling its requirements today.

A Message or a Grouch?

If you honestly want to better the world, all you need do is *meet the tests it gives today and tomorrow it will listen to you.*

If you have a message and not just a grouch you are willing to submit to the world's acid test—*the test of personal achievement*—to earn the chance to deliver that message.

If you do not care enough for it thus to sacrifice yourself you can't blame the world for not being willing to sacrifice *itself.*

Money-Making and Self-Confidence

The world is a big place. There are millions of people in it. To win their belief in you, you must set them the example. You must believe in yourself ❧❧

We know a young man who has been trying for months to get a situation.

He is always turned down.

He does not understand why.

We could quickly tell him. He doesn't *talk like* a success. He doesn't *look like one*. He is trying to dispose of something which he does *not present in an attractive form*. People feel that he **doesn't believe in himself.**

Your prospective employer, buyer, or friend is watching you with an "eagle eye." He is looking for victory in your face—not defeat; he is looking for *evidences of ability*—not incompetence.

Everyone is after 100 per cent men and women and will take no others if they can possibly avoid it.

Every employer wants cheerful, optimistic, self-confident employees around him; men and women who bear the earmarks of efficiency; who are *good walking ads for his business.*

His trained eye tells him instantly whether you are going to impress his customers as a *winner* or a *loser.*

To get a really good position you have got to convince your prospective employer that he will have a prize in you.

Don't Sit Back

One of the greatest American writers has said: "Talent is sure of a market, but it must not cower at home and expect to be sought out.

"There is a good deal of cant in the criticism of the aggressive, forward-pushing man. It is complained that retiring men of worth are passed over with neglect.

"Sad as this is for the retiring, worth-while people, it usually happens that the forward pushing men have the *qualities of activity and accomplishment* without which worth is *a gold mine that can't be operated.*

"A barking dog is sometimes more valuable than a sleeping lion."

Uses of Ego

"Egotist" is the term you like to apply to the man who has done more than you. As a matter of fact, it is probably egotism that has enabled him to climb up where he is.

If his being there worries you so much that *you find yourself constantly accusing him*, the chances are that *your own egotism* is at the bottom of your resentment.

Jealousy is the confession of your own inferiority.

A certain amount of good healthy egotism is necessary to the success of any man or woman.

As long as it is not used to belittle others it is a good thing. It acts as the spur without which few great steps would have been made in the world's progress ❧❧

No Time to Hunt You Out

In these busy days men have no time to hunt about in obscure corners for retiring merit. They find it more effective to take a man at his own estimate till time shall prove otherwise.

The world admires manliness and courage. It admires womanliness, and true womanliness in this day and age means the self-confidence of a winner.

The world has little use for the timid, whether male or female. It passes by the self-effacing people who have an air of apologizing for living.

What Is Wanted

Leaders in every walk of life must have lieutenants who *also know how to lead.* Therefore, they select for the big places the people of *positive mentalities*—men who *radiate victory*, who express confidence in themselves: who can *get things done*, who can *put big undertakings through, who have the triumphant attitude.*

Charles M. Schwab, an expert in estimating and measuring ability, says: "I have great faith *in those who have great faith in themselves.* I know that the men who fear themselves are not fit for responsibility."

Trust Yourself

If you look as though you had lost your nerve, your faith in yourself, your self-confidence, no one is going to give you a responsible position. It is human to have faith in those *who have faith in themselves*

Regardless of whether you have yet won out or not, if you are a conqueror in your own mind, if you have a victorious manner, OTHER PEOPLE WILL BELIEVE IN YOU.

On the other hand, if you tag yourself with things bespeaking uncertainty, doubt or timidity, the law will work the other way.

Thousands of seekers for positions go after them in a half-hearted, dejected, discouraged way. They are convinced at the beginning that they are not going to get the place.

Why They Got No Raise

Scores of able young men and women among our students have asked why it was they never got a raise in salary. In almost every instance they admitted they made the request **expecting to be refused.**

The psychology of it is this: the world demands that you make a success of your own individual personality before asking it to take you into partnership in *its* business.

It sees that the timid, self-conscious man is **not succeeding with his own mental attitudes** and automatically concludes that he is not a safe risk.

The World Steps Aside

The world makes way for the self-confident man ❦❦

There is no use trying to stop him. No use opposing him ❦❦

If you dam up his efforts in one direction he gathers force and breaks over in another.

No enemy or enemies are great enough to forestall him. **Only the weak can be beaten by their enemies.** The self-confident man plows through everything and reaches his goal.

Your Two Partners

The next step essential to success is:

Think of yourself as two persons—the real you who has *given the orders* for doing this thing, and your other self which must *carry them out.*

Let this second self see that you expect it to carry out these orders. Never rescind those orders as long as you wish to accomplish that particular thing.

Let your other self see you are **expecting it to deliver the goods.** When it whines and wants to beg off don't listen. It is your weaker nature, your lazy self— that negative part that acts as a drag to the ambitions.

A True Story

Right here let us tell you of something which has been most effective in the life of one of America's most successful women. She said:

"I learned how this lazy other self was always trying to get out of work. I discovered it could think up the most plausible excuses for justifying me. I found that if I left any loopholes open it always came around whispering how some other time would do. 'Let's just take today off-one more day of vacation won't do any harm, and we'll make it up tomorrow.'

"I found that this enemy Inertia was trapping me into neglecting the things I had set out to do, and after a few years I was dismayed to realize that I had allowed it to cheat me out of my greatest desires 🙪🙪

"So, I devised a trap for it.

"Knowing that this weaker side of myself would continue to creep in whenever I was off guard and beguile me away from the task which my better self had set, I forestalled its activities.

"Whenever I had fully decided to do something worthwhile, and while my best self was still at the helm, I made whatever arrangements were necessary to **compel me to accomplish it.**

For instance, if I decided to write a book on a certain subject, I announced that fact to my classes, giving the exact date when it would be available 🙪🙪

"When I had prepared a new lecture, I compelled myself to give it by engaging the hall, paying a deposit, and advertising in the newspapers.

"The greatest undertaking of my life I literally forced myself to engage in.

"After years of study and preparation I still delayed, giving myself the excuse that I needed more time in which to make the final arrangements.

"At last, I determined to inaugurate it on a certain date. Ordinarily I would have given myself about four years to put on the last finishing touches. As it was, I gave myself exactly six months to the day.

"Hundreds of times in those six months my weaker self-rebelled, declared I could never do it, that I had set myself to do the impossible.

"Sometimes when the task threatened to overwhelm me I almost succumbed, but the size of the stake I had deliberately placed in the balance was so great I dared not.

"I now know that the development, soul-growth and inspiration I gained from delivering exactly what I had contracted, on the exact date, was worth more than anything the other three years of half-work could have given me.

"From that day to this my weaker self has never been able to re-establish herself in her old place of dominance. To be sure, she comes back. She comes back with the same excuses and sometimes they sound very seductive. But I control the situation now.

"I still tie myself up with contracts, agreements, advertising and other inexorable task masters ❧❧

"I still have my weaker self but it knows its place." ❧❧

You can teach yours to know its place. You can rise above it, conquer it and put it beneath your feet.

How to Make Yourself Win

Take for granted that you have energy, courage, enthusiasm and self-confidence to do what you want to do.

Place yourself in a position where others expect you to do it, and when the time comes you will find yourself in possession of the qualities with which to do it.

Stop thinking poverty if you wish to attract prosperity. Refuse to give a place in your mind to the things you fear.

Stop Focusing On Fear

The man who focuses his mind on expectations of failure, poverty, who banishes ambitions, hope, and gives full sway to doubt, fear and timidity, inevitably ***brings these things to pass.*** No power on earth can make such a man succeed. Nor can any power on earth keep down the man who holds the ***opposite*** expectations of himself.

Think the things you want; furthermore, ***don't be afraid to want.*** There is a world of difference between wishing and wanting. The ***"wishers"*** usually fail while the ***"wanters" win.***

Pinching Your Life

Thousands of lives are made small, pinched and narrow because people are afraid to desire, to fling out their longings, to visualize them.

Instead of believing we can get the thing we desire we spend our time exaggerating our restrictions and limitations.

All men and women who have climbed to the top of life's ladder climbed up ***mentally*** first.

Most failures are due to the fact that people are not willing to do their part toward making their dreams come true. They wish "to have their cake and eat it too,"—to take things easy and have the good things of life drop into their laps by magic.

The Door of Opportunity

Opportunities always come, doors are always opening, the road is always made clear to the man or woman **who trusts and works.** They seldom open in just the way or at just the time he expects, but they open often to far **bigger** things than he ever dreamed of. Nothing comes to the weak, doubting heart save the crumbs of existence.

Someone has said, "The world is a whispering gallery which sends back the echo of your own voice." Someone else has said, "It is a mirror which reflects the face it sees in it." If we frown it frowns, if we laugh it laughs back.

Exaggerating Our Weaknesses

One of the saddest things is this fact, that most people measure themselves by their weaknesses instead of by their **strength.** They estimate themselves at their worst instead of their best. They seem to feel that the vision they see of themselves in self-confident, optimistic, exalted moments is a figment of the imagination and not their real selves 🙠🙠

Very few people realize how much self-confidence has to do with accomplishment. Most people do not realize that it is a creative force. It is not only a creative force but one of the greatest in man-so great, in fact, that man accomplishes in almost **exact proportion to his self-confidence.**

Keep your eyes and ears open.

Never tell any one of your educational deficiencies. Get knowledge. If you did not get a college education don't brood over it. Educate yourself 🙠🙠

Don't let the fact that you lack social standing get your goat." Instead of regretting that you are not the son of a "best" family of "blue bloods," start a best family of your own; a family of such good red blood that it will never need traditions to bolster it up.

Positive and Negative

Take a positive attitude toward everything in your life. Think and act POSITIVELY, never negatively 🙠🙠

Instead of saying, "I can't afford this," and "We mustn't do that because we are going to need this money next year," spend all that is necessary, and say, "I will make more for next year."

Those who are constantly retrenching, who deny themselves here, pinch themselves there, and skimp somewhere else, *are always poor.* They take the poverty attitude, the negative attitude toward life 🙠🙠

Determine to make more money next year. Force yourself to make more. Save a certain percentage always but *don't take it all out in saving.*

Don't Frivol all the Time

Another trouble with us is that we do not concentrate. We want things but we do not want them badly enough to keep working for them. Our thoughts are truants. They go off on vacations. They want to play, to frivol, to enjoy themselves. And we wind up where the enjoyer always winds up—at the small end of things.

Why We Don't Get Rich

We wish for riches, station, fame, but we refuse to pay for them. We do not want to earn them. We want them to fall into our hands.

We know many young women, and middle-age ones, too, who say, "How I long to have plenty of money, a beautiful home; I adore lovely things, exquisite possessions, handsome cars and elegant clothes. Why can't I have them?"

The answer is simple. They can't have them because they do not earn them. Only one woman in millions has them fall into her lap via marriage.

Thousands of American women are earning them. Female brains are making fortunes today and more will make them in the future.

If you really want money, and want it badly enough, that desire will kindle the fire necessary to burn your way to it.

Don't waste your time longing to lure a money making male into marriage. It costs too much. It usually costs a great deal more than it is worth. Almost any rich wife will tell you so, especially if she married him **after** the riches were made.

The Natural Leader

People fail to get what they desire because they do not desire it hard enough. The man or woman of strong desire draws everything toward him that he wants because a strong desire compels action and action is what gets everything.

The man of strong desire draws not only things but people to him. People instinctively fall in with his suggestions. They feel drawn toward him. Nothing can withstand him.

Keep the fire of your desire burning bright and fierce or it will not awaken you to action. Allow yourself to want things with all your might and they will in turn cause you to do the things that bring them to you.

The Man of Will

We have heard much about the "magnetic" individual; the kind of man who has the power to attract people to him.

These men invariably possess great will power. They are the active, energetic, forceful men. All great minds possess this kind of energy *to a marked degree* ❧❧

The Hunger for Achievement

There are those who have been able to work their will upon the mass of people. These men are seen to possess a strange power, but very few understand it. It forces and compels; nothing can stand in its way. No one ever did anything or got anything who was not filled with a strong, hungry desire ཤྲུ

The man who feels and hungers for achievement will make mighty efforts to satisfy that hunger ཤྲུ

Around you every day you see people who go to any length to satisfy the hunger for food.

The great men of the world have felt the same way in their hunger for achievement.

All "feelings" that incite one to action of any kind are forms of desire. Without desire the world would cease absolutely from action.

Desire and Renunciation

Preceding every action is desire, either conscious or unconscious. Those who make a virtue of renouncing desire, who claim to have "conquered desire absolutely," are acting in response to desire of a more subtle form. They are expressing a desire **not to do** other things.

All renunciation is the result of desire, just as its opposite is the result of desire.

This is a fundamental natural law. "Lack of desire" to do a certain thing is another way of expressing **a desire to pursue an opposite course.** And so it goes. Desire is at the root of every action and every refraining from action. **Nothing has ever been done, created or manifested without desire** ཤྲུ

Keen Desire Finds a Way

A keen, ardent desire will cut away the undergrowth from the path of success. It will attract you to the things and the people necessary for its gratification. ***It will bring you directly or indirectly to the circumstances, conditions and environments necessary to your success.*** It will seldom bring you by the exact route you anticipated, but the destination is the important thing.

Will Power and Money

The man of will power is wanted everywhere. The world is crying for him.

One of America's most famous financiers said recently, "I have a twenty-five thousand-dollar-a-year jobs for men of will power."

When asked what he meant by a man of will power he said, "I mean a man filled with the force of action; a man who is determined; who keeps his mind on an object just as a machinist keeps his chisel on the metal, makes it bite in deeper and deeper ***until the desired impression is made***" ❧❧

Cultivate fixity of purpose.

To hit a target you must see it.

To arrive at any point you must keep your eye on it and go straight toward it.

Fix your will upon ***what you want***, hold it there, and move toward it in as straight a line as possible ❧❧

Turn the spotlight of concentration on it and every faculty will gravitate toward its accomplishment just as the eyes of an audience follow a spotlight on the stage.

The people or objects outside the rim of the spotlight are not seen.

You can develop concentration to the point where inimical or opposing matters ***will not be felt.*** The spotlight of concentration illumines your aim, magnifies it, brings it out with such distinctness that other things do not tempt you.

Concentrate!

To accomplish a thing, "Cut off both ends and set it afire in the middle," is the way one author puts it.

The sun shining on a newspaper is sufficiently diffused—spread out—that nothing happens but concentrate that sunshine down to the area of a pinpoint and it will ***burn a hole through it.***

To get anything in this world you have got to ***burn holes through the things that intervene.*** You must center not only your body but your mind on the thing.

Stop Wasteful Thinking

All outside activities dissipate your energies. Stop losing power in the thinking of wasteful thoughts. You cannot stop the ceaseless activities of the mind but you can direct them into the channels that are worth while.

Stop yourself sometime when you are hurrying in a crowded day's work. Note what an inner whirlwind of excitement is going on inside your mind.

Walter Dill Scott of Northwestern University said, "In studying the lives of contemporary business men two facts stand out pre-eminently. The first is that they have accomplished what to most of us seemed impossible. Such men appear as giants in comparison with whom ordinary men sink to the size of pigmies.

"The second fact is that ***they never seem rushed for time.*** The secret of it seems to be that they require less time because their concentration accomplishes in one hour what ordinary men take three hours to do."

Apply Your Energy

That there is an enormous lack of proper application of energy in the lives of most men is an undoubted fact.

What you need is ***not more power but more sensible application*** of the powers you are wasting.

You often hear a big business man spoken of as "a human dynamo." We are impressed by his power, by his ability to turn out a stupendous amount of work in a short time. We exclaim at his capacity for carrying in his mind the details of so many projects and wonder how he can accomplish so much in so many directions; how he can pull the strings of so many enterprises without ever getting lost in the maze of details.

Keep to the Point

If you will look you will find the explanation. Nearly every word and act of this man is ***straight to the point.*** The business of the day is carried along in a steady drive. This is invariably the mark of the big man.

The man who chatters, clatters and flutters usually imagines he is getting over a lot of track, but he wastes far more steam than he uses.

New Ways Come

By keeping your physical and mental energies ***riveted on what you want to do*** there can be no insurmountable obstacles.

You may not be able to do it just the way you planned, but new conceptions, new ways and methods will come to you just as surely as you keep your desire and concentration.

By concentration we do not merely mean the keeping of your ***surface mind*** on your ideal. We mean building it so deeply into your subconscious that if awakened from the soundest sleep in the middle of the night you could tell—before you were entirely awake *what that aim was.*

Ask any successful man if his success came about in the manner in which he expected and he will say, "No. Many of the specific plans I laid were frustrated, but my determination *brought from somewhere* other plans that served my purpose as well or even better than those I had originally conceived."

Your Untapped Reserves

The reason for this is scientific. In every brain there are millions of unused brain cells the "reserves." ❧❧

The average person, because he never places himself in jeopardy, never has the use of these reserves.

But the man who calls upon his brain for them not only finds them responding to his needs but *develops new ones.*

Brain building is the development or growth of the brain cells in any special region of the brain.

As you know, the brain is divided into sections or areas, each one being the seat of some particular faculty. These areas are the same in all human beings ❧❧

It has long been recognized that these brain centers could be developed. In some instances specialists, whose work demanded great concentration, developed that particular brain area to such an extent that changes in the outward shape and size of their skulls was apparent. The bony structure of the skull accommodates itself very gradually and in ordinary cases the change is not noticeable.

Brain-Building

It has been demonstrated many times that a man may literally make himself over mentally.

All that is necessary is that he devote the same degree of attention, patience and work to the subject that he would if he were attempting to develop some physical muscle.

The processes for developing mental and physical muscle are almost identical *exercise, practice, persistence* ❧❧

You can increase any brain area, therefore any ability, faculty or talent.

Earnest desire, intensified by visualization, stimulates the brain centers, sends the blood to that area and eventually *causes the creation of new cells.*

The mere general longing for success is not enough. *Nothing indefinite will ever get you anywhere.* You must have definite interests clearly defined. The mind must be given something specific, important and *tangible* to work on.

New details will be needed constantly. But if you really *want* this thing, your desire will furnish those details.

A Mental Five and Ten Center

Concentration has been the secret back of every invention. If Thomas A. Edison had given his attention to the thousand little odds and ends that the rest of us do, how far do you think he would have climbed?

How far do you think Any other big man would have gone? ❧❧

How far do you think you are going to get, if, instead of conducting a specialty shop, you run a mental *five-and-ten-cent store?*

Don't Waste Time

Do not make engagements that will dissipate your powers. Be jealous of your time.

Franklin said, "Dost thou love life? Then do not squander time for that is the stuff life is made of." &

Give money to the needy; be generous with your worldly goods, *but give no man your time!*

Do not allow yourself to waste time, strength or energy reading things that cannot serve your purpose &

Over the desk of a prominent executive in New York City is this statement, "Be brief. The man who steals my time is the most dangerous thief" &

Conserve Your Energy

Conserve your energy for the accomplishment *of your great aim in life.* Do not become narrow, selfish or self-centered but let everyone know that you are on the road to *some place in particular* and that you do not intend to loiter along the way. Any one worth while will respect you all the more, for every one worth while is doing the same himself.

Turn Your Back on Poverty

There is only one sure way to get away from poverty and that is to TURN YOUR BACK ON IT &

Begin this minute by putting the poverty thought *out of your mind.* Get the *poverty expression* out of your eyes, the *poverty tones,* out of your voice, the *poverty limpness* out of your handshake &

Mentally, physically, and spiritually erase, as far as you can, marks of poverty. Erase the marks of poverty from your clothing, your surroundings, your bearing, your environment as a whole &

Don't Give Up

All solids and metals have what is called a melting point. At a certain temperature they tend to liquefy. The test of you is *your melting point*, the place **where you are ready to quit,** to lie down, to give up.

Nearly every rich man will tell you that every big triumph was preceded by places of dark discouragement which, had he heeded them, would have marked his end.

The difference between the poor man and the rich man is usually just that. One gives up when things look dark. The other **shuts his eyes, grits his teeth, clenches his fists and hangs on!**

SO HERE THEN ENDETH "HOW TO UTILIZE YOUR MIND THROUGH THE SCIENCE OF PRACTICAL PSYCHOLOGY," BEING THE FOURTH LARGE EDITION OF THIS WORK; BY ELSIE LINCOLN BENEDICT, THE FIRST TEACHER IN AMERICA TO CONDUCT PUBLIC LECTURE COURSES ON THE SUBJECT OF PRACTICAL PSYCHOLOGY; ALSO BY RALPH PAINE BENEDICT, COLLABORATOR AND COMRADE ❦ PRINTED AND MADE INTO A BOOK BY THE ROYCROFTERS AT THEIR SHOPS WHICH ARE LOCATED IN EAST AURORA, ERIE COUNTY, STATE OF NEW YORK, IN THE YEAR NINETEEN HUNDRED AND TWENTY-TWO

This edition was reprinted in the United States in 2026 by the Benedict School of Opportunity, LLC. A fourth-generation Benedict family preserving the works of Elsie Lincoln Benedict and Ralph Paine Benedict.

We thank you for supporting the continuation of their legacy.

This reproduction remains true to the original layout and design, with gentle editorial updates such as clarified punctuation and attribution of previously anonymous quotes, where applicable.

www.ingramcontent.com/pod-product-compliance
Lightning Source LLC
Chambersburg PA
CBHW030428160726
47991CB00005B/1638